# Keeping Together in Time

# KEEPING TOGETHER IN TIME

## *Dance and Drill in Human History*

### WILLIAM H. McNEILL

Harvard University Press

CAMBRIDGE, MASSACHUSETTS · 1995

*Library of Congress Cataloging-in-Publication Data*
McNeill, William Hardy, 1917–
    Keeping together in time  :  dance and drill in human history  /
William H. McNeill.
        p.  cm.
    Includes index.
    ISBN 0-674-50229-9 (alk. paper)
    1. Rhythm—Psychological aspects.  2. Rhythm—Psychological
aspects—Cross-cultural studies.  3. Dancing—Psychological aspects.
4. Dancing—Psychological aspects—Cross-cultural studies.
5. Movement, Psychology of.  I. Title.
BF474.M37  1995
306.4'84—dc20

95-8794
    CIP

# Preface

THIS LITTLE BOOK has had a difficult parturition. It started with my encounter with military drill in 1941, but real investigation waited until the 1990s, when I was invited to give the Lee Knowles Lectures at Trinity College, Cambridge. These lectures are supposed to deal with military history, and preparing them invited or compelled me to concentrate on the military side of the phenomenon I set out to investigate. Since the lectures were also expected to be few in number, I chose to restrict attention to examples of how emotional bonding among particular human groups aroused by dance and/or drill could plausibly be supposed to have changed the course of the world's history. This boiled down to prehistoric cooperation in the hunt, followed by Sumerian spearmen, Hebrew prophets, Greek hoplites, Maurice of Orange, and Hjalmar Ling. It made an odd assortment.

At the invitation of Professor Johan Goudsblom I visited Amsterdam immediately after Cambridge and summarized my lectures before a group of anthropologists and sociologists. The Dutch were mildly interested, as Cambridge historians were not, but remained skeptical. My most articulate critics disliked the military bias of my presentation and pointed out that I had overlooked ordinary community dancing, which was obviously the most important expression of the form of human behavior I was interested in. They also made clear that human evolution was a controversial domain where intruders like myself ventured at their peril.

These encounters in Cambridge and Amsterdam persuaded me that reconsideration was in order. Yet the belief that I was onto something that others had missed kept pricking me on. Moreover, informal conversations at various institutions where I was invited to lecture on other subjects often homed in on what was I "going to do next?" And with more hardihood than prudence I regularly replied by sketching my notions about what I came to call "muscular bonding," that is, the human emotional response to moving rhythmically together in dance and drill. Such encounters eventually convinced me that this *was* what I was going to do next. In the course of one such conversation, a youthful faculty member at the University of Calgary proposed the title *Keeping Together in Time* for my projected history. The delightful double meaning of "time" built into that wording struck me as elegantly apt; and I am genuinely grateful, even though I am not now able to name her or thank her personally.

After the Amsterdam talk it was clear to me that I would have to explore human evolution more carefully, if I were to give plausibility to my hunch about the importance of keeping together in time for permitting full humanity to emerge from prehuman populations. I also realized that restricting examples to supposedly world-changing instances was rhetorically and practically wrong-headed. Community dancing on festival occasions was obviously the most important way in which this human propensity found expression, and always had been. Moreover, religious manifestations of muscular bonding were both more various and more widespread in the historic record than military instances, owing to the way cavalry had dominated Eurasian battlefields through most of recorded history, making close-order drill ineffective.

Reshaping my approach along these lines, in turn, called for further reading; and a generous invitation from James Billington, Librarian of Congress, allowed me to use the facilities of that magnificent institution in the autumn of 1993 to look into human evolution on the one hand and religious history on the other. Supplemental visits to Yale University's libraries, and one brief but valuable foray into the stacks at Wesleyan University during the process of actual composition, allowed this essay to assume its final form. I hereby thank the authorities who so generously gave me access to these collections. Without their help I could not have worked out my ideas as fully as they are here set forth.

Yet I must close this preface with a note of warning. What follows is by no means a completed historical inquiry. Sampling is erratic, especially in Chapter 4, dealing with religious manifestations of muscular bonding. And the chapter on human evolution relies, regrettably but inevitably, on inference from and analogy with chimpanzee behavior as recently observed. Most surprising (to me) is the further fact that I could not discover really helpful experimental studies of what happens within the human body when people keep time together for prolonged periods of time. I am haunted by the notion that somewhere in the vast body of articles reporting results of psychological and physiological experimentation answers to my naive questions must exist. I scamped other dimensions of the subject as well, making no effort to read widely in anthropological literature, for instance, where descriptions of community dancing most certainly abound. My efforts to sample the writings of dance historians and of European folklorists were also abbreviated, largely because what I did find was of little or no value for my inquiry.

By comparison, what I have to say about the military side of the theme is more firmly based on the scholarly work of others. The questions I ask are different; and my effort to pursue the subject across the whole of Eurasia—and to sample, insofar as one can, what happened in other parts of the earth where the horse did not alter the pattern of warfare—is unusual. But when it comes to facts upon which I base my conclusions, Chapter 5 is in a class by itself, largely because my own previous reading and research prepared me to treat that part of the theme with far greater authority than I can claim for the other, and, I now believe, historically more important expressions of the human capability I tried to investigate in this essay

What follows, therefore, is a reconnaissance, exploring an aspect of human behavior that is of far greater importance for our social life than ordinary consciousness and words themselves can readily acknowledge. By definition, most of what I have to say is not directly attested in written sources, since it deals with emotions that were not expressed verbally by those who felt them, though their actions were nonetheless altered by what they felt. Yet to suppose that what was not written down and preserved for modern inspection therefore did not operate among human beings in times past is obviously false. What scholars can hope to do is to study the records of the past with an alertness to what we know or surmise about human responses to keeping together in time. I have not done so here, save in a few instances, relying instead on what others have reported about village communities, religious sects, and companies of soldiers.

The thesis of this little book is simplicity itself. Moving our muscles rhythmically and giving voice consolidate group solidarity by altering human feelings. This, I believe, is well attested by experience, though little discussed by any learned discipline. It follows that this sort of human behavior deserves to be investigated by historians, sociologists, psychologists, physiologists, and a host of other specialists with far more pertinacity and acuity than has yet been brought to bear on the subject. The vagaries of intellectual history are such that these experts may or may not take up the challenge. In the meanwhile, the brief exploration of human responses to keeping together in time that follows invites readers to reflect on their own personal responses to dance, drill, and song and to wonder about the importance of the phenomenon in general.

March 1995                                        Colebrook, Connecticut

# Contents

Illustrations follow page 86

# Muscular Bonding

IN SEPTEMBER 1941 I was drafted into the army of the United States and underwent basic training in Texas along with thousands of other young men. Supplies were short. We boasted a single (inoperative) anti-aircraft gun for the entire battalion, so that practical training on the weapon we were supposed to master was impossible. Consequently, whenever our officers ran out of training films and other ways of using up time, we were set to marching about on a dusty, gravelled patch of the Texas plain under the command of an illiterate noncom. A more useless exercise would be hard to imagine. Given the facts of twentieth-century warfare, troop movement in the rear was a matter of trucks and railroads. Close-order marching within range of machine guns and rifles was a form of suicide. All concerned realized these simple facts, yet still we drilled, hour after hour, moving in unison and by the numbers in response to shouted commands, sweating in the hot sun, and, every so often, counting out the cadence as we marched: Hut! Hup! Hip! Four!

Treasured army tradition held that this sort of thing made raw recruits into soldiers. That was enough for our officers and the cadre of enlisted men who were in charge of our training. But why did young Americans not object to senseless sweating in the sun? At the time I was too busy getting used to totally unfamiliar routines and social relations to ask the question,

much less reflect upon it. What I remember now, years afterwards, is that I rather liked strutting around, and so, I feel sure,
did most of my fellows.[1] Marching aimlessly about on the drill
field, swaggering in conformity with prescribed military postures, conscious only of keeping in step so as to make the next
move correctly and in time somehow felt good. Words are
inadequate to describe the emotion aroused by the prolonged
movement in unison that drilling involved. A sense of pervasive
well-being is what I recall; more specifically, a strange sense of
personal enlargement; a sort of swelling out, becoming bigger
than life, thanks to participation in collective ritual.

But such phrases are far too analytical to do justice to the
experience. It was something felt, not talked about. Words,
in a sense, destroy what they purport to describe because they
limit and define: in this case, a state of generalized emotional
exaltation whose warmth was indubitable, without, however,
having any definite external meaning or attachment. The
strongest human emotions—love, hate, and fear—are ordinar-
ily triggered by encounters with other persons or particular
external circumstances, and the emotion in question helps us
to react successfully. But the diffused exaltation induced by
drill has no apparent external stimulus. Instead, marching
became an end in itself. Moving briskly and keeping in time
was enough to make us feel good about ourselves, satisfied
to be moving together, and vaguely pleased with the world
at large.

Obviously, something visceral was at work; something, I
later concluded, far older than language and critically important in human history, because the emotion it arouses constitutes an indefinitely expansible basis for social cohesion among
any and every group that keeps together in time, moving big
muscles together and chanting, singing, or shouting rhythmically. "Muscular bonding" is the most economical label I could
find for this phenomenon, and I hope the phrase will be understood to mean the euphoric fellow feeling that prolonged and

rhythmic muscular movement arouses among nearly all participants in such exercises.[2]

In later years I had occcasion to recall and reflect upon my response to close-order drill anew. In particular, when writing *The Pursuit of Power,* I concluded that the modern superiority of European armies over others was largely due to the psychological effect of the sort of close-order drill I had experienced. Maurice of Orange had introduced incessant drill to the Dutch army in the 1590s, and it spread across Europe like wildfire in the ensuing half century.[3] One obvious reason was that well-drilled troops were more efficient in battle; but an additional advantage was that it became safe to arm even the poorest classes, pay them a pittance, and still expect and secure obedience. The emotional resonance of daily and prolonged close-order drill created such a lively *esprit de corps* among the poverty-stricken peasant recruits and urban outcasts who came to constitute the rank and file of European armies, that other social ties faded to insignificance among them. Such troops soon came to constitute a cheap, reliable instrument in the hands of European statesmen and generals. Within two centuries, they carried European power around the globe; and in time of domestic disturbances, European soldiers were even willing to fire upon their own kind—at least most of the time.

Reflecting on my odd, surprising, and apparently visceral response to close-order drill, and recalling what little I knew about war dances and other rhythmic exercises among hunters and gatherers, I surmised that the emotional response to drill was an inheritance from prehistoric times, when our ancestors had danced around their camp fires before and after faring forth to hunt wild and dangerous animals. It was easy to suppose that by rehearsing what had been done before and would be done again in pursuing and killing their prey, ancient hunters' actual performance in the field gained precision. If so, better success was assured; survival became easier. I concluded that rigorous selection in favor of groups that kept together in

4 ··· KEEPING TOGETHER IN TIME

time had led to genetic transmission of this capability, which then was inadvertently tapped by Maurice of Orange and innumerable drill sergeants ever since.

Such a hypothesis means that emotional response to rhythmic movement in unison ought to be universal; its manifestations pervasive; and its importance in history enormous. But in fact close-order drill is conspicuous by its absence in most armies and military traditions. From a world perspective, indeed, the way Greeks and Romans and then modern Europeans exploited the psychological affect of keeping together in time was an oddity, not the norm of military history. Why should Europeans have specialized in exploiting the extraordinary possibilities of close-order drill? More important, how has the phenomenon of muscular bonding manifested itself across the centuries and among innumerable different societies?

The specifically military manifestations of this human capability are of less importance than the general enhancement of social cohesion that village dancing imparted to the majority of human beings from the time that agriculture began. Two corollaries demand attention. First, throughout recorded history, moving and singing together made collective tasks far more efficient. Without rhythmical coordination of the muscular effort required to haul and pry heavy stones into place, the pyramids of Egypt and many other famous monuments could not have been built. Second, I am convinced that long before written records allowed us to know anything precise about human behavior, keeping together in time became important for human evolution, allowing early human groups to increase their size, enhance their cohesion, and assure survival by improving their success in guarding territory, securing food, and nurturing the young.

That may perhaps count as a political expression of the emotional force of muscular bonding; and festive village dancing was political too, smoothing out frictions and consolidating fellow-feeling among the participants. But such descriptions are unduly analytical, since in the depths of evolutionary time as well as in agricultural villages of historic ages, social, religious, political, and economic aspects of community life presumably constituted an undifferentiated whole.

In ancient civilized societies, where different groups went their separate ways, older forms of muscular bonding continued to exercise their influence in everyday rural settings; but, in addition, specifically religious manifestations of such bonding became an important way of creating emotionally vibrant primary groups within which human lives found meaning and direction. Then, in modern times, political and military expressions of this human capability separated out from more generalized social and religious contexts. Their importance was enormous, as the historic role of close-order drill for modern armies and of calisthenics and parades for nationalist movements of the nineteenth and twentieth centuries amply attest in every part of the earth.

Our television screens show continuing, pervasive manifestations of the human penchant for moving together in time. American football crowds, South African demonstrators, patriotic parades, and religious rituals of every description all draw on the emotional affect of rhythmic movements and gestures. So of course do dancing, military drill, and the muscular exercises with which, it is said, workers in Japanese factories begin each day. Yet, so far as I can discover, scientific investigation of what happens to those who engage in such behavior remains scant and unsystematic. Psychologists and physiologists have not been much interested. Extreme states, especially the onset of trance after appropriate warm-up by song and dance, have excited considerable discussion. But precise measurement of neural, hormonal, and other physiological changes incident to trance is conspicuous for its absence; only a few, crude experiments have sought to measure what happens within the brain when eyes and ears are subjected to rhythmic external stimuli. Despite two bouts of library research, I found no physiological studies of human emotional responses to rhythmic muscular movement in groups, nor even to choral singing.

Yet some things seem reasonably sure. The primary seat of bodily response to rhythmic movement is apparently situated in the sympathetic and para-sympathetic nervous systems.[4] These nerve complexes are involved in all emotions; but exact paths of emotional excitation by the sympathetic nervous system and of compensatory restoration of bodily homeostasis by the para-sympathetic nervous system are not understood. Various hormones excreted by the pituitary gland and by other organs of the body play a role;[5] so do the hypothalamus, the amygdala,[6] and the right side of the cerebral cortex.[7] Only after filtering through these levels of the brain does excitation derived from rhythmic muscular movement and voicing reach the left side of the brain, where our verbal skills are situated.[8]

With such a pathway of response to rhythmic muscular movement, it is no wonder that our words fumble when seeking to describe what happens within us when we dance or march. The initial seat of excitement is far removed from our verbal capabilities. It centers instead in those parts of the nervous system that function subconsciously, maintaining rhythmic heartbeat, digestive peristalsis, and breathing, as well as all the other chemical and physiological balances required for the maintenance of ordinary bodily functions.

The critical fact, however, from my point of view, is that whatever happens at a subconscious level in response to rhythmic stimulation from movements of the big muscles results in a diffused state of excitement that is definitely pleasurable at the conscious level. Why this is so remains obscure.[9] Experiments have shown that rhythmic stimulation of eye and ear enhances brain waves in the cortex, and when the periodicity of the light or sound stimulus is close to natural rhythms, the two tend to match up.[10] But the experiments that produced this result were conducted in a laboratory, where the subjects sat or lay down in order to allow electrodes, wired to their heads, to transmit brain-wave impulses to a recorder. Obviously, cerebral response to flashing light and rhythmic sounds under such circumstances proves nothing about actual dancers' reaction to rhythmic kinesthetic stimulation. Experimental exploration of exactly what the sympathetic and para-sympathetic nervous systems do when we dance or march together seems never to have been attempted, perhaps because it would be difficult (or impossible?) to carry through without altering the dance or damaging the bodies of those subjected to such experiments.

Reflecting on these matters, it has occurred to me that rhythmic input from muscles and voice, after gradually suffusing through the entire nervous system, may provoke echoes of the fetal condition when a major and perhaps principal external stimulus to the developing brain was the mother's heartbeat. If so, one might suppose that adults when dancing or merely marching together might arouse something like the state of consciousness they left behind in infancy, when psychologists seem to agree that no distinction is made between self and surroundings. It seems plausible to suggest, therefore, that prolonged and insistent rhythmic stimuli may restore a simulacrum of fetal emotions to consciousness. Obviously no one knows, and experimental validation seems intrinsically impossible.

All the same, the idea accords nicely with what anthropologists and dance historians have to say about the state of mind induced by keeping together in time. Thus, for example, when an anthropologist questioned ritual dancers in Greece, they explained that they felt "light, calm and joyful."[11] Another observer reports that hunters and gatherers of the Kalahari desert say: "Being at a dance makes our hearts happy."[12] More commonly, anthropologists rely on their own vocabulary and intutition, as A. R. Radcliffe-Brown obviously did when he wrote of the Andaman islanders: "As the dancer loses himself in the dance, as he becomes absorbed in the unified community, he reaches a state of elation in which he feels himself filled with energy or force immediately beyond his ordinary state, and so finds himself able to perform prodigies of exertion."[13]

A contemporary dance historian offers a more economical description, referring to "boundary loss, the submergence of self in the flow,"[14] though what the flow may be she does not say. Subhuza II, a Swazi king who had studied anthropology in England before assuming his royal duties, was a bit more down to earth when, in 1940, he explained what happened among his subjects: "The warriors dance and sing at the Incwala [an annual festival] so that they do not fight, although they are many and from all parts of the country and proud. When they dance they feel they are one and they can praise each other."[15]

"Boundary loss" is the individual and "feeling they are one" is the collective way of looking at the same thing: a blurring of self-awareness and the heightening of fellow-feeling with all who share in the dance. It matches my own recollection of what close-order drill felt like, so I take this to be the characteristic alteration of consciousness that sets in as the rhythm of muscular movement takes hold, and before prolonged or heightened exertion brings on ecstatic states when awareness of others fades away and excitement concentrates within the self. Very likely trance is provoked when restorative responses, triggered by the para-sympathetic nervous system, take over dominance from the excitatory reponses of the sympathetic nervous system.[16] Ecstasy induced among adepts by physical exercises, and the encounter with spirits or God that ecstasy was commonly believed to bring in its train, add a complex, extra dimension to what I hold to be the more generally significant social bonding that rhythmic moving together arouses among ordinary people. Seeming contraries, they are indissolubly connected and both have had great importance throughout human history.

Obviously, the impact of marching in unison is much more subdued than the emotions aroused among dancers. Perhaps for that reason, military writers have been remarkably inarticulate about the emotional effect of drill. To be sure, Maurice de Saxe, Marshal of France (d. 1750), explained how fatigue should be countered:

> Have them march in cadence. There is the whole secret, and it is the military step of the Romans. . . . Everyone has seen people dancing all night. But take a man and make him dance for a quarter of an hour without music and see if he can bear it. . . . Movement to music is natural and automatic. I have often noticed while the drums were beating for the colors, that all the soldiers marched in cadence without intention and without realizing it. Nature and instinct did it for them.[17]

Nature and instinct still operate in the twentieth century and affect thoroughly urbanized, highly educated persons, as my own response to close-order drill in 1941 illustrates, and as testimony from the distinguished military historian, Sir Michael Howard, confirms. Having spent many youthful hours on the drill field, he recalled that "Drill developed group cohesion to a very high degree."[18] But military writers have preferred to justify continued resort to close-order drill, after it lost its practical meaning on the battlefield in the 1840s, by making unconfirmed assertions about how drill inculcates automatic, unthinking obedience. Before then, the obvious, intended effect of improving the effectiveness of volleyed fire was all the justification that drill, and still more drill, needed; and only Maurice de Saxe seems to have taken note of one aspect of its emotional side effects.

A few observers of modern warfare have emphasized the strong attachment to "buddies" that allows armies to function as they do. Sociologists studying World War II experience discovered that what kept men fighting was not propaganda nor words of any kind, but an intense fellow-feeling for those close at hand and sharing imminent, obvious danger.[19] A reflective soldier's ruminations expressed the phenomenon more vividly:

> Many veterans who are honest with themselves will admit, I believe, that the experience of communal effort in battle, even under the altered conditions of modern war, has been the high point of their lives. . . . Their "I" passes insensibly into a "we," "my" becomes "our," and individual fate loses its central importance. . . . I believe that it is nothing less than the assurance of immortality that makes self sacrifice at these moments so relatively easy. . . . I may fall, but I do not die, for that which is real in me goes forward and lives on in the comrades for whom I gave up my life.[20]

Obviously, this sort of merger between self and the surrounding group, attained in the heat of battle, is analogous to the "boundary loss" attributed to dancers. It is also induced by close-order drill, though only in attenuated measure. If so, drill, dance, and battle belong together. All three create and sustain group cohesion;[21] and the creation and maintenance of social groups—together with resulting rivalries among groups—constitute the warp and weft of human history.

Yet historians and social theorists, like psychologists and physiologists, have paid little attention to muscular manifestations of group solidarity. We are captives of language for our explanations, and words do not capture the visceral emotions aroused by keeping together in time. People have always danced but seldom wrote about it, and almost never tried to analyze what they felt while moving rhythmically together. Sources are therefore scant to nonexistent.

This does not mean that the phenomenon of muscular bonding was unimportant. Quite the contrary. This book explores a few of the historically important manifestations of group formation through rhythmic muscular movement in hope of persuading others to consider the phenomenon with the seriousness it deserves. Group consolidation through dance was, perhaps, critical in separating our remote ancestors from other protohominid species; and dance certainly operated throughout historic times to maintain village communities and innumerable other human groups.

Let me therefore discuss the tangled theme of human evolution and the possible role that keeping together in time may have played in that story before taking up some of the historic manifestations of this odd sort of human behavior.

# Human Evolution

COMMUNITY DANCING occurs only among humans, if by that phrase we mean a form of group behavior whereby an indefinite number of individuals start to move their muscles rhythmically, establish a regular beat, and continue doing so for long enough to arouse euphoric excitement shared by all participants, and (more faintly) by onlookers as well. Moreover, community dancing is very widespread among human societies, and it takes place under a great variety of circumstances, with many different meanings attached to the performances. Indeed, community dancing, together with marching and singing or shouting rhythmically is, like language, a capability that marks humans off from all other forms of life. I propose to argue that learning to move and give voice in this fashion, and the strengthened emotional bonds associated with that sort of behavior, were critical prerequisites for the emergence of humanity.

Common speech does not recognize the uniqueness of human dancing behavior. That is because our word "dancing" embraces solo exhibitions and muscular movements associated with courtship, as well as shared group exercises. Thus when male birds court their mates with stylized muscular displays, we call it dancing. And when a bee communicates the location of a new food source to its fellows in the hive by means of stylized body movements, we call that dancing too. But such performances do not involve moving together and keeping time, whereas excited groups of humans often keep time spontaneously, and solemn exercitants do the same in innumerable institutional settings whenever marching, dancing and singing are customary.

At first blush, the way birds, fish, dolphins, and perhaps other animals sometimes move in flocks or schools—each individual maintaining more or less the same position with respect to its neighbors—looks more like the human style of dancing together. Such schooling requires coordination of movement so that any change of speed or direction spreads almost instantly; otherwise the formation would break up in confusion. But such coordination does not require keeping time to a regular beat. Humans establish a common rhythm for dance and drill by planting their feet on the ground simultaneously (or very nearly so); but birds and schools of fish have other (presumably visual, and for dolphins also vocal) ways of relating to one another that do not involve the maintenance of a regular beat. Such behavior is unique to us, even though approximations to human dancing have been observed among our nearest relatives, the chimpanzees.

Much can be learned about dance and the possible course of human evolution from recent observations of bands of chimpanzees. Modern study of captive chimpanzees attained a new level of sophistication when, in 1913, the Prussian Academy of Sciences established colonies of three species of apes, including a few chimpanzees, in the Canary Islands and sent a young psychologist, Wolfgang Kohler, to study them. In 1917 Kohler published a famous book, translated as *The Mentality of Apes*,[1] proving that chimpanzees could solve problems and invent new ways of getting at food by using simple tools for the purpose. Psychological study of captive chimpanzees has continued ever since, with various foci of investigation. For my purposes, the most interesting are recent studies of shifting patterns of individual dominance among a group of chimpanzees in the Arnhem zoo.[2]

Observation of chimpanzee behavior took a new turn in 1960, when Jane Goodall began her study of a band that remained in its native habitat in the Gombe Game Reserve, Tanzania. She was sponsored by Louis Leakey, the famous discoverer of early hominid remains at Olduvai gorge; and part of her purpose from the start was to look for parallels with early hominid behavior. To do so she decided to give each individual member of the band a name, and recorded his or her behavior for years on end in such a way that individual life careers and kinship ties became apparent. After 1970, rather suddenly, the dynamics of relationships with other bands also began to emerge, though only dimly, since critical boundary clashes commonly took place beyond the reach of direct human observation.

Goodall only overcame the natural wariness of the chimpanzees she studied by feeding them bananas, initially on a daily basis. This means that she, as well as almost all subsequent students of chimpanzee behavior at other sites in the open, have recorded somewhat modified behavior, as against what must have prevailed before human beings started to impinge so closely on their lives.[3]

Watching and recording what the animals did, without interference other than that created by a new source of food and the human presence itself, meant that conditions of life for the chimpanzees were not as artificial as those of a zoo; and, to counteract too much dependence on an abnormal food supply, the feeding stations were redesigned and equipped with remote controls in 1969 so that individual animals could be rationed to a few bananas once a fortnight.[4] That more nearly resembled the irregular rhythm by which chimpanzees gather wild fruits in different places at different times of year. As expected, diminished food supplies dispersed the crowd that had formed around the feeding station, but human observers tried to keep in contact with the chimpanzees who went off to seek food. Keeping up with them was not easy, and individuals or whole groups often disappeared from human view for a while. Nonetheless, by following roving chimpanzees through the forest, observers were able to record new, aggressive (and all too human) aspects of chimpanzee behavior in 1970–1972, after the supply of bananas at the feeding stations had been cut back to a more nearly "natural" level.

Observation in zoos and in the modified wild conditions of the Gombe Game Reserve showed that chimpanzees exhibit close analogues to the individual movements of human dance. What ethologists call "display behavior" involves bipedal posture, rhythmic foot stamping, and hooting noises, together with emphatic arm and facial gestures that look much like human dance. On occasion, several animals engage in simultaneous display behavior. Here, for instance, is Goodall's account of how adult male chimpanzees react to a thunderstorm: "Sometimes when the first drops hit them they begin a display, wildly and rhythmically swaying from foot to foot, rocking saplings to and fro, stamping the ground. This spectacular performance we call a 'rain dance.'"[5] Since the participants were not moving to a common rhythm, this was not dancing by human standards, even though individual movements were so much like those of human dancers that Goodall called it so.

Yet from her account it appears that the individual feats of one performer were sometimes imitated by another. Perhaps this raised the level of excitement beyond anything generated by solo displays; but of course no one can really know what the animals felt, nor be sure why thunderstorms trigger such behavior. Human observers commonly connect display behavior with ambiguous situations in which the performer is not sure what to do. As one expert puts it: "The elaborate tantrum-like dances of chimpanzees and gorillas occur not only for the relief of tension, but often seem to be intended as a challenge to some rival or to impress the rest of the group, being accompanied by the noise of stamping, hitting and yelling."[6]

Human dancing, too, may relieve tension and impress or challenge others, but its distinctive capability of enhancing group solidarity probably depends on keeping time together for a prolonged period, thus translating individual discharge of anxiety into collective catharsis. Moving rhythmically so as to establish a regular beat has never been observed among chimpanzees living in the open, even though individuals in at least one band did sometimes produce drum-like sounds by lying down and beating hind feet against a resonant tree buttress![7] Everything needed for human dance therefore seems at hand among our closest animal relatives, except the habit of keeping together in time.

With a little coaching from humans, chimpanzees can in fact cross that divide and learn to dance just as we do. In a famous passage, Wolfgang Kohler described how the animals he studied at Tenerife in the Canaries, 1913–1917, would sometimes start to circle a post in their compound, until

> The character of their movement changes; they no longer walk, they trot, and as a rule with special emphasis on one foot, while the other steps lightly; thus a rough approximation of rhythm develops, and they tend to "keep time" with one another. . . . A trusted human friend is allowed to share in these games with pleasure . . . and sometimes I needed only to stamp rhythmically, as described, around a post, for a couple of black figures to form my train. If I had enough of it and left them, the game generally came to an abrupt end. The animals squatted down with an air of disappointment, like children who "won't play any more" when their big brother turns away. I first took part in this game after it had taken place without me hundreds of times.[8]

But not, one may surmise, before other human attendants assigned to the task of collecting the animals and establishing them at Tenerife had shown them how to dance by doing so themselves, and attracting the sort of imitation that Kohler himself subsequently provoked.

Chimpanzees can imitate many forms of human behavior, as efforts to raise them like human children have shown, and psychological experiments have turned up a number of striking perceptual and behavioral convergences.[9] This is not altogether surprising, since the differences between human and chimpanzee DNA are so small that geneticists calculate that the two stocks diverged only about six or seven million years ago.[10] It thus appears that chimpanzees are indeed our first cousins, far closer to humans than any other species. Among the most striking evidences of this kinship is the fact that power relationships within human groups closely resemble the politics of chimpanzee bands, as recently described by careful observers. This point deserves to be illustrated in somewhat greater detail.

After the banana supply at the feeding stations in Gombe was cut back in 1969, the band divided up. A group of seven males left the feeding station and set up a new band in adjacent territory. Previously, the dominant male of the Gombe band had been repeatedly challenged by the animal that became leader of the secessionists. Then, in the course of the next two years, raiding parties from the Gombe band attacked and probably killed each of the male secessionists, thus re-annexing the territory and the females the secessionists had briefly controlled. Raiders ambushed single males, and apparently numbers always were decisive, although in at least one case the victim was not killed outright. But he presumably died soon after human observers sighted him for the last time, since he appeared to be seriously crippled by his wounds. These raids were not directly observed so that exactly how the larger band destroyed its rival cannot be reconstructed in detail. But war to the death, or something suspiciously like it, apparently broke out; and as a result the smaller group ceased to exist within about two years of its formation.[11]

Some years before it thus became obvious that conduct around the feeding station at Gombe did not exhaust the repertoire of chimpanzee behavior, observers had begun to try to follow small roving parties of the animals—both at Gombe and elsewhere—in hope of learning more about their ways of living in the forest. These efforts soon made it clear that relations between adjacent bands differed drastically, depending on sex. Females in estrus often wandered across territorial boundaries to mate with males from an adjacent band. Sometimes they returned, more often they stayed with the new band.[12]

Males, however, stayed within the community of their birth. They regularly patrolled the boundaries of their territory in groups of varying size, every so often probing beyond its limits to see what reaction they might provoke from a neighboring band. When more or less equal numbers encountered one another, the intruders withdrew in haste; but when a band encountered a single male, lethal attack ensued often, perhaps always. Boundary patrols were noisy while moving within the home territory, thus warning off intruders. On penetrating hostile ground, however, they became quiet and moved stealthily—ready to flee from serious opposition or to attack any isolated male they might run across.[13]

A related pattern of behavior among male chimpanzees impels them to form alliances with each other that alter across time, creating a pattern of dominance and submission that connects all the males of the band into an unstable, cooperative whole. Gestures of dominance and submission are codified; within the band individuals very seldom actually fight with one another. But confrontations that test established relations of dominance and submission occur frequently; and the alpha male, to whom all others submit, is repeatedly assailed by would-be successors to the top rank. Alliances with other males are decisive in defining dominance. Leaders of subordinate groups spend much effort in cultivating support by grooming their followers, attracting new ones, and sharing meat or other precious food with them.[14] The alpha male does the same thing, and is compelled to spend more time and effort cultivating others than subordinate males bother doing. Cooperation thus becomes the key to dominance. The alpha male, in short, is a politician, just as leaders of roving parties that go off to look for food and patrol territorial boundaries are also politicians on a smaller scale.

Observation both in zoos and in the open shows that the hierarchy of dominance among males depends on fluctuating individual relationships between clusters of leaders and followers. The reign of a particular alpha male only lasts from three to seven years, because accumulated grudges and slights break up his following and allow a successor to consolidate new alliances and thereby establish his right to exact submissive behavior from all the males of the band.[15]

A key aspect of the male chimpanzee dominance hierarchy is that success depends on the number of supporters who are prepared to follow a given leader. Numbers prevail by tacit understanding; and in test confrontations between rivals, the males present line up on one side or the other, or stand apart as a third force of neutrals. Almost always, gestures make fighting unnecessary. As a result, individual size and strength are not in themselves decisive. What matters are the individual political skills that attract and retain followers, and probably also the emotional ties arising in infancy among the sons of the same female.[16]

Given the instability and complexity of male relationships, it is perhaps not surprising to learn that the largest number of adult males ever recorded as belonging to a single band in the open is sixteen.[17] It is instructive to realize that the secession at Gombe occurred among only fifteen allied and competing males. The seven who departed left eight behind; yet that difference in numbers (together, presumably, with individual differences among the animals concerned and in the solidarity of the rival followings) was sufficient to allow the larger band to exterminate the smaller in about two years.[18]

This sort of political structure, with its shifting alliances, is "exceedingly unusual"[19] and is, perhaps, shared only with humans and a smaller species of ape known as bonobos. It presumably arose because cooperating gangs could easily attack and kill lone males, so that selection came to favor the cultivation of mutual bonds among males and the muting of sexual[20] and other forms of competition among them. At the same time, unstable male solidarity within each of the resulting bands automatically created hostile relations with neighboring bands. This is no more than expected, since the evolutionary advantage which male cooperation conferred was to connect reproductive success with collective defense (or expansion) of a home territory within which females and the young could thrive.[21]

A further aspect of the male interaction that holds chimpanzee bands together is that all the band members seldom assemble in one place. Instead, what has been called "fission-fusion sociality" prevails, whereby wandering groups, usually of four to six animals (mostly but not exclusively male), scatter out across the band's territory and yet can readily recognize one another as belonging together when they meet again. Males travel in groups and are seldom alone; whereas much of the time individual females have only their dependent young around them. Like males, adult females sometimes confront one another, using the same gestures of dominance and submission. But the dominance hierarchy among them is seldom tested because females concentrate mainly on their own offspring—where the mother's dominance is assured—and only occasionally interact directly with other adult females.

Chimpanzee politics show obvious similarities with human behavior. Like chimpanzees, small human communities often have hostile relations with neighbors and defend a fairly well defined home territory from encroachment by outsiders with all the force at their command.[22] In prehistory, cooperation among men, especially for hunting and war, was more obvious than cooperation among women, who spent much of their time and effort on the nurture of children. Even today, hunting and gathering communities often break up into small parties at the times of year when food supplies are lowest, only to reassemble and renew social ties with their fellows on more bountiful, festival occasions. And of course humans dance at such festivals, keeping together in time, and thereby actuate the social bonds discussed in the previous chapter. Perhaps because of that, human societies are far larger than chimpanzee bands, and routinely incorporate many more than sixteen adult males in cooperative hierarchies.

Given what we know and surmise about human reactions to rhythmic movement and chimpanzees' apparent capacity for learning to dance, it would be interesting to see what the effect of dancing together might be on chimpanzee patterns of dominance and submission. Since chimpanzees share with us the parts of our nervous system that respond most immediately to rhythmic movement, it is probable that very similar emotions would arise, strengthening solidarity and dissipating the frictions that plainly do exist within the bands as now constituted.

Perhaps the rivalries that led to the split at Gombe might have been diminished or even dissolved entirely had the animals concerned known how to dance together. Indeed, I would suppose that existing limits on the size of chimpanzee bands would be greatly enlarged if chimpanzees learned to keep time together and could thus arouse emotions like those that human beings feel when they dance. And since numbers count so decisively in the border encounters that define each band's territory, it follows that a larger band with stronger cohesion among its members would have an enormous advantage in the ongoing competition for territory and breeding success.

This, indeed, is exactly what I surmise did happen among our ancestors. By engaging in prolonged group display behavior and discovering the delight of keeping together in time (perhaps helped by the beat of sticks against the ground or some more resounding surface), they could begin to feel, as the Swazi king said of his warriors in 1940, that "they are one and can praise each other."[23] Praise had to wait upon words, which came later; but the expanded emotional solidarity that dancing together arouses must have conferred an important advantage on those groups that first learned the trick of keeping together in time. So great, indeed, was the advantage, that other hominid groups presumably either learned to dance or became extinct. That is why all human societies dance today and have done so throughout the recorded past. Chimpanzees did of course escape extinction in the tropical forests of Africa without learning to dance. But that is not surprising if, as seems probable, our protohuman ancestors learned to dance only after they had moved out onto the open savanna, ceasing to compete directly with forest dwellers.

THE COURSE of human evolution is much disputed, and experts seem not to have considered dance as a factor in the process. The idea therefore lacks learned support, and before the hypothesis can be adequately evaluated, it needs to be fitted into received notions about how human beings emerged from our prehuman and protohuman predecessors. This is treacherous ground, however, for skeletal fragments and other archaeological traces so far discovered do not allow the experts to establish a clear line of descent. All the same, ever since Thomas Huxley pioneered the inquiry by publishing *Evidence as to Man's Place in Nature* in 1863, enormous ingenuity has been expended on fragmentary but ever-increasing data. Changes in our own society have also affected how the evidence is interpreted. Thus, for example, feminists recently challenged older views about the importance of hunting in human evolution, without, however, winning anything like a clear victory for their views. Despite such perturbations, increasing information from more and more sites has tended to establish consensus on some key points, even though new finds, like those Louis and Mary Leakey made in Olduvai gorge a generation ago, can always alter the picture anew.

Contemporary understanding of human evolution begins the story with the development of bipedalism in Africa between five and ten million years ago among creatures labelled *Australopithecus*. Quite divergent skeletal remains suggest that separate australopithecine species existed, occupying different landscapes perhaps, and/or succeeding one another in time. One variant, dated to about 1.75 million years ago, was discovered by the Leakeys. They dubbed their find *Homo habilis*, because of an enlarged brain pan and flaked stone tools associated with the skeletal finds, and argued that *Homo habilis* constituted a distinct species, ancestral to humankind. Others disagreed; and confusion about the earliest skeletal fragments that deserve to be labelled *Homo* continues to prevail.

Agreement becomes firmer about identifying other bones, coming from several different sites in Asia and Africa, as *Homo erectus*. These creatures began to roam on the African savanna about 1.8 million years ago, and subsequently extended their range to parts of Asia and Europe starting about a million years ago. In due course *Homo erectus* was succeeded by *Homo sapiens*—a species that probably arose in Africa perhaps as much as 200,000 years ago—and proceeded to expand its range all round the earth, reaching the Americas between 30,000 and 15,000 years ago and penetrating the last considerable area of habitable land as recently as 1000 years ago, when humans first occupied New Zealand.[24]

But such a schema, based on skeletal differences, does not illuminate all the important aspects of human evolution. In particular, there appears to be a substantial gap in time between the appearance of the earliest skeletons classified as *Homo sapiens* and the onset of a radical change in behavior that began about 40,000 years ago, and sustained an amazingly rapid expansion into diverse climatic regions on the one hand, and a suddenly accelerated rate of innovation in tool shapes and materials on the other. The succession of new sorts of stone, bone, and antler tools certainly suggests that human beings began to show an unprecedented capacity to invent new ways of doing things. And we may confidently infer that a long succession of such inventions, starting about 40,000 years ago and continuing until the present, allowed humans to divert an ever-larger proportion of the earth's energy flows to serve their needs and wishes.

The historic human career as we know it thus began some 40,000 years ago, when human culture—that is, learned behavior—overtook genetic mutation as the major variable operating upon earth's ecological balances; it seems reasonable to suppose that the principal instrument of this extraordinary transformation was the emergence of fully articulated language. That is because human language opened up new possibilities of classifying and reacting to the external world, and permitted really large-scale cooperation (now literally global) on the basis of accumulating knowledge and experience.

But even if, as many linguists now believe, grammatical structures are somehow wired into the neural connectivities of the left cortex of the human brain, it is unlikely that fully articulated language sprang from nowhere. Other, cruder ways of communicating must have existed among our ancestors long before the shift to articulated speech and thought that probably took place about 40,000 years ago. Indeed, chimpanzees and monkeys have a restricted but meaningful repertory of vocal calls, and they do interact through facial and bodily gestures.[25] Some of their facial gestures—and associated meanings—are shared with humans, notably the smile.[26] It therefore seems entirely likely that *Homo erectus* communities had some sort of protolanguage at their command, perhaps analogous to the forms of language that are common today to infants under two years of age, to specially trained apes, and to adults who resort to pidgin when communicating with speakers of another, unfamiliar language. Whether all pidgin languages conform to a common pattern remains a matter of dispute. Some linguists argue that pidgin is a sort of protolanguage, comprising any number of terms, with meanings established initially by gesture and context but lacking the grammatical structure and syntactic expressions necessary for the construction of sentences. Many practical tasks and everyday transactions can be accurately handled by use of pidgin, but such languages characteristically evade abstract discourse and so cannot create the subjective world (related to, but largely independent of, the everyday world of external things) which characterizes fully articulated human languages.[27]

The capacity to conceive alternatives through logical and imaginative play with words is presumably what allows human beings to invent new ways of behaving, both among themselves and in relation to the natural world around them. Abstract ideas, in other words, started to direct actions along different paths in diverse environments and situations and in various types of human communities, as soon as fully articulated language arose. The consequences were enormous, introducing a new, cultural level of evolution to the earth—a process that radically transformed the biosphere in a mere 40,000 years, and, through industrial pollution, has begun to alter the atmosphere and hydrosphere as well.

But just as the emergence of articulate language seems to have been the principal catalyst for the remarkable earthly career of *Homo sapiens,* the less extraordinary but still remarkable career of *Homo erectus* can plausibly be connected with a similar mutation of communicative behavior—using something like pidgin at the verbal level, backed up with shared emotional solidarities induced by dance.[28]

If one supposes that, after biological evolution had introduced *Homo erectus* to the African savanna, some of them learned to keep together in time by coordinating their display behavior, and persisted in moving together rhythmically for a long enough time to arouse euphoric emotional excitement similar to what I experienced on a Texas drill field in 1941, it is easy to imagine far-ranging practical consequences analogous to the consequences that probably flowed from the invention of fully articulated language among bands of Homo sapiens something like a million years afterwards. Let me explore some of the probable, plausible consequences of learning to dance together.

The first and most fundamental effect of such a change has been mentioned already. Moving together rhythmically for hours on end can be counted upon to strengthen emotional bonds among those who take part—women as much as men. Far larger bands than any existing today among chimpanzees or other great apes could therefore come into being, with immediate advantages for mutual protection and the expansion of territory at the expense both of competing species and of smaller bands of Homo erectus that did not learn to dance. Border patrol and the sort of guerrilla and ambush against alien males that operate among chimpanzees today would produce this result very quickly. What we may think of as the human scale of primary community, comprising anything from several score to many hundreds of persons, thus emerged, thanks to the emotional solidarities aroused by keeping together in time.[29]

A second and no less significant consequence of dancing together was that two basic strategies of survival—the search for food and the nurture of the young—became more efficient. This involved a differentiation of daily activity between the two sexes greater than prevails among chimpanzees today. Stronger bonding among males made cooperative hunting more effective, while among females stronger bonding meant that nurture of the young could be better assured by being shared more widely than is the case among modern chimpanzees. In particular, when improved skill in the hunt allowed men to kill large animals regularly, sharing meat with women and children became easy and normal. Innumerable other consequences flowed from the habit of sharing food within more or less stable family circles—so much so that a distinguished school of paleoanthropologists has argued that food-sharing was fundamental to the emergence of humanity from protohominid ancestors.[30]

Chimpanzees do hunt small animals, but among groups that have been observed in the open, meat constitutes only about three percent of their caloric intake.[31] It is nonetheless highly regarded, and chimpanzees at Gombe devoted considerable effort to cooperative hunting in groups of two to as many as nine (usually male) adults. A successful hunter was often approached by others as he consumed his prey, and induced to share it with them through "tolerated scrounging."[32]

Hunting on the African savanna asked for rather different skills from those which chimpanzees employ in their forested habitat. At Gombe chimpanzees hunt young monkeys for the most part[33] and rely on surrounding the prey, often by treeing it, cutting off escape routes, and then waiting, sometimes for more than a hour, until one of the hunters succeeds in seizing and beating the captive to insensibility before biting into it. Such tactics are quite effective. Between 1960 and 1970 forty-six successful hunts were observed within a radius of 150 yards of the feeding stations at Gombe, while in thirty-seven instances the prey escaped.[34]

Our ancestors on the African savanna developed different ways of killing. First of all, bipedalism freed human hands to use sticks as clubs and prods, and human inventiveness presently elaborated them into spears and javelins armed with stone heads. This vastly extended the reach of the arms and fingers upon which chimpanzees rely to seize their prey. In addition, hairlessness and the remarkable abundance of sweat glands, which distinguish us from almost all other animals,[35] endowed human beings with an extremely efficient cooling system. In the heat of the day naked hunters, thanks to their sweat glands, could persist in a long-distance chase when far swifter prey would collapse from heat stroke, for even the most strenuous panting cannot keep bodily temperatures anywhere near normal after prolonged exertion. In Australia, for instance, kangaroos develop incapacitatingly high body temperatures when aborigines pursue them on foot for one to two hours, and smaller animals, like hares, can be overtaken more quickly than that when they faint from excessive body heat.[36]

Perhaps because of the risks of overheating, contemporary predators on the African savanna, except for wild dogs, hunt only at night or in the coolness of dusk.[37] It looks, therefore, as though when our human ancestors shed their body hair and started to sweat, they opened up a new niche for themselves as diurnal hunters. (Incidentally, it is probably no accident that dogs were the first species to be domesticated, since among terrestrial animals[38] they alone shared and competed with our ancestors in daytime hunting.)

Obviously, bones and stones do not tell when sweating and nakedness became the human norm, but no one can doubt that this was a fitting adaptation for life on the savanna, where the tropical sun beats down relentlessly. Since *Homo erectus* inhabited savanna lands in Africa, it is tempting to suppose that sweating, and the daytime hunting that it facilitated, became standard among *Homo erectus* populations in Africa before some of them moved into Asia.[39]

For a while in the 1970s and 1980s a school of paleoanthropologists minimized the role of big game hunting in human evolution. Bones of large animals found at ancient camp sites could be attributed to scavenging; and the preponderance of gathering—of which scavenging was a special case—in the human past could be affirmed, less on the basis of definite evidence than because it gave equal or superior importance to provisioning by females.[40] But others insisted that *Homo erectus* bands owed much of their success to proficiency in killing large animals.[41]

The truth is that nobody really knows how *Homo erectus* bands actually behaved; and nobody can know exactly when killing big animals began to give males regular access to more meat than they could possibly consume on the spot. That did happen eventually. Chemical analysis of Neanderthal skeletons recently showed that their diet was predominantly carnivorous;[42] and perhaps the same techniques can be applied in future to *Homo erectus* skeletons to discover the balance of their dietary intake.

Pending such researches, it seems best to settle for the observation that if *Homo erectus* bands learned to consolidate sentiments of social solidarity by dancing together, their hunting would have become more efficient. Hunters could, like modern pygmies,[43] rehearse their past successes through dance, mimicking how they ambushed the prey, drove it into a trap, or merely prodded it out of its burrow. Such re-enactments, combined with enhanced emotional solidarity provoked by the rhythms of dance, would—like military drill in Old Regime armies—make actual performance in the field more predictable. And, as was also true of such armies, the emotional bonding induced by dance would allow each individual hunter to play his part more bravely, standing firm when an encircled animal tried to break out, and using his stick in time-tested ways to turn it back or head it towards a trap prepared in advance.

All this is imaginary, of course. No one is ever likely to know for sure how *Homo erectus* bands hunted. Yet there is one indirect line of reasoning to support the notion that hunting became more important among that species. Simply by dint of their place in the food chain, carnivores require larger territories than herbivores of equal body weights. Is it then merely accidental that *Homo erectus* extended its range from the African savanna across much of Asia and Europe about a million years ago? Or was this a response to, and indication of, an increasingly carnivorous diet and the corresponding need for larger territories? Again, no one can know for sure; but some experts have suggested such a connection.[44]

A word of warning is appropriate at this point of the argument. It is probably wrong to emphasize dancing in isolation from other factors, as my effort to insert it into the debate over human evolution tends to do. One ought rather to think of a situation in which more precise cooperation among larger numbers began to have the effect of expanding the supply of food, so that any and every behavioral change that strengthened cooperation enhanced survival. In such a situation, the diffuse emotional solidarity aroused by dancing together, and the more specific utility of rehearsing how to cooperate in the hunt, could come into their own as efficient ways of enlarging the food supply. Once hit upon, such behavior would quickly spread, since bands that did not dance would suffer crippling handicap in competition with those that did.

Perhaps, too, genetic selection in favor of individuals and groups that enhanced social solidarity most vivaciously through dancing may have altered neural linkages of the sympathetic nervous system in a fashion analogous to the ways our left cerebral cortex may subsequently have altered its structure to accommodate (and reward) the development of fully articulated language. Food supply and breeding success were obviously critical for survival—always. Behavioral changes presumably acted selectively upon genetic variations, rewarding some and penalizing others.

My suggestion therefore boils down to the proposition that among our ancestors the habit of dancing together probably began to have strong positive effect on survival before articulate language arose; and this trait most probably established itself among *Homo erectus* bands on the African savanna, at a time when hunting larger and larger animals began to assume a greater place in our ancestors' food supply.

THE EFFECT upon the female sex of stronger bonding through dance was probably just as important as its effect among male hunters. Chimpanzees learn the arts of life almost exclusively from their mothers. A mother's death automatically means death for the infant. Males play almost no role in nurturing the young, and after weaning the young start to feed themselves, learning which fruits, leaves, and shoots to pluck by imitating how their mothers do it. Food-sharing occurs, but is usually confined to specially attractive tidbits such as meat, and is part of a network of reciprocity that includes grooming and the gestures of dominance and submission that play so prominent a part among male chimpanzees.[45] Finally, sexual promiscuity appears to be part and parcel of the male hierarchy of dominance and submission, inasmuch as the alpha male allows other adult males to have unhampered sexual access to estrus females. Any other policy, presumably, would break up his following and inhibit male cooperation in defense of the band's territory upon which survival depends.

The human pattern of food-sharing and sexual pairing is quite different. When and how it arose is as mysterious as other aspects of protohominid and early human behavior. But a key element, surely, was to connect food-sharing more closely with paternity—something entirely lacking among chimpanzees. Obviously, when hunters began to return more or less regularly with extra meat to give to females and their young, new patterns of food-sharing could arise—trading off the high food value of meat for the perhaps greater dependability of vegetable foods collected by females and the young. The eventual upshot was family structures like those familiar in all human societies today, whereby sexual relations and food-sharing tend to coincide, and both sexes contribute to the nurture of the young long past the age of weaning.[46]

Advantages of this pattern of nurture are obvious. Even a loose specialization of labor between hunting and gathering meant that a broader spectrum of foods could enter the diet, and seasonal shortages of any one sort of food became less critical. Simultaneously, lengthening dependence of the young extended opportunities for teaching and learning. Moreover, the fact that meat has high nutritive value meant that its consumers had more leisure time in which to elaborate the arts of life by playful, inventive behavior and to teach whatever worked well to others.[47] This must have helped *Homo erectus* to adapt to the different climates and landscapes that bands encountered when they left the African savanna. On top of all these advantages, better nutriment perhaps made viable genetic changes that increased longevity.[48] This in turn began to permit grandmothers and grandfathers to participate in nurturing the young, and allowed old men and women to become living storehouses of information about once-in-a-lifetime emergencies and occurrences that required unusual responses.

In short, new human patterns of nurture meant that storage and retrieval of information was markedly improved by exploiting the potentialities inherent in extended youth and prolonged old age. This, at bottom, was what made *Homo erectus* bands so successful in expanding their territorial range across diverse climatic zones as no other large-bodied species was able to do. I do not know that dancing was essential to that success, but it is plausible to suppose that it was. Assuredly, emotional solidarity within larger communities, sustained by keeping together in time, would also improve and expand the storage and retrieval of information, simply because larger numbers of individuals would begin to take part in all such information networks.

Thus it appears that human evolution may have involved two critical transformations, both of which centered on improved communication. First, the dance and the emotional linkages that it established; then, articulate speech and the symbolic linkages which fully developed language allowed. Both may have started among quite limited populations, beginning as one-time events and spreading in somewhat the same way that more recent transformations of human society have also spread around the world from distinct loci of origin among comparatively small populations. The industrial revolution is the most obvious such case; but many others—agricultural diffusions from a variety of places or the electronic innovations of our own day—conform to a similar pattern.[49]

The speculative element in such a reconstruction is enormous. No one is ever likely to know for sure what enhanced behavioral and communicative capabilities did for *Homo erectus* or for the first stages of *Homo sapiens'* career. But emphasis on communication, at the emotional as well as at the symbolic level, has the virtue of fitting smoothly into subsequent, historically recorded mutations of human society, which have always turned on changes in patterns of communication and contact across cultural and other boundaries. This was the organizing theme of my principal work, *The Rise of the West: A History of the Human Community,*[50] and I need not rehearse the detailed evidence there adduced in support of this general proposition.

No one doubts that what makes us human is our participation in communication networks—linguistic primarily, but supplemented mathematically and digitally at one end of the spectrum and gesturally and emotionally at the other. It is therefore entirely plausible to suppose that successive improvements in the carrying capacity of such networks constitute the principal landmarks of human evolution and of human history as well, simply because it was this that permitted our ancestors to cooperate more and more effectively in larger and larger groups so as to extract more and more food and other forms of energy from the world around us.

If one contemplates the spectrum of communication as it exists today—ranging from the arcane digitalized output of computers to the ancient and still mysterious emotional contagion aroused by moving and giving voice together in time—it becomes obvious that the muscular, emotional level of communication has been generally neglected. Students of human evolution have overlooked it; so have historians. The following chapters aspire to do something to repair that omission, more by way of sketching some illustrative examples than with anything like a comprehensive history. But plainly, if the emotional effect of keeping together in time is as I claim, the influence of such exercises on human societies must be pervasive and powerful, however inarticulate, little noticed, or seldom recorded.

# Small Communities

The archetypical form of dance among humans occurs on festival occasions, when almost everyone in the community joins in and keeps going for hours on end. Such events are almost universal among small, independent communities, whether these sustain themselves by hunting and gathering or by agriculture or by a combination of both. The effect on participants is what we have learned to expect. Heightened emotion finds its principal expression through making all concerned feel good about themselves and those around them. Shared emotion of this vaguely euphoric tone, in turn, binds the community more firmly together and makes cooperative efforts of every kind easier to carry through.[1]

This, in fact, was the really important function of dancing in human history. It is hard to write about, however, because it was so commonplace. Ordinary people danced as a matter of course, and seldom had occasion to record the fact or notice its effects. Changes undoubtedly did occur in all manner of detail: dress, musical accompaniment, muscular performance, all were subject to invention and elaboration. Ideas about what was being celebrated and why were no less changeable across the centuries. Historians of dance have done what they could to weave the very fragmentary information provided by written and visual sources into a coherent account of how styles of dance played diverse functions in different societies across time, but what happened at the small community level before modern times largely escapes them, simply because it was not recorded, being too much a matter of course.[2]

Moreover, the occasional descriptions (and denunciations) of popular dancing that dance historians have gleaned from the literary record say nothing about the emotional residues of keeping together in time; yet these, I claim, constituted the historically important contribution of dancing to social cohesion and group survival. But the universality—or near universality—of festival dancing suggests that the custom must have had some utility. The extravagant expenditure of bodily energy involved in community dancing—sometimes for days on end—was costly, after all. Muscular effort expended in dance might have been reserved instead for economically productive work, or for guarding home territory against neighboring enemies.

No doubt, the emotional excitement and general sense of well-being that dancing induced were enough to attract individual participants. But private pleasure, by itself, does not seem enough to explain the phenomenon. Humankind has not escaped biological selection pressure, after all; what looks like extravagance and waste could scarcely be so general if it did not have a positive effect on collective survival by consolidating common effort in crisis situations. The connnection is most obvious in war dances, which prepared fighting men for the risks of ambush and battle;[3] but the more general consolidation of sentiment among all members of the community, male and female, old and young, that community-wide dancing induced may well have been more important in maintaining everyday routines and all the forms of cooperative behavior needed for the effective conduct of community affairs.[4]

DOES COMMUNITY DANCING have any recoverable history? If one accepts the argument of the preceding chapter, emerging *Homo sapiens* may be presumed to have inherited the habit of dancing from *Homo erectus* ancestors, whoever they may have been. But even if that is so, for something like four-fifths of the temporal career of *Homo sapiens* on earth nothing is knowable about dance behavior. Only the Late Paleolithic, between 18,000 and 12,000 years ago, leaves some ambiguous evidence for human dancing: it is the human figure portrayed in the Trois Frères cave, often referred to as The Sorcerer. He is shown in a crouched position, wearing an animal disguise, and his legs are splayed. This may indeed represent some sort of ritual dancing. The art of this French cave is unusual because other human or half-human figures that may also be dancers appear on its walls, along with the more usual portrayals of game animals. But since each figure is separate, community-wide dancing is not attested to at Trois Frères; and how to interpret what the individual figures are doing is not clear.

An unambiguous representation of group dancing appears in a cave painting of indeterminate date near Palermo in Sicily. It shows a circle of seven men dancing together, each with one leg lifted into an almost exactly parallel position. Yet seven males keeping time together do not constitute a community-wide celebration; and the artist may have portrayed expert performers rather than ordinary people. At any rate, in the center of the circle, two acrobats appear to be turning somersaults in mid-air, a feat requiring unusual, and perhaps semiprofessional, expertise.[5]

The earliest plausible portrayal of community dancing that I have run across comes from Minoan Crete about 1500 B.C., in the form of the fragmentary Harvester Vase. This shows vivacious rejoicing at a harvest festival. Open mouths, together with hands holding musical instruments as well as agricultural tools, indicate that singing was very much part of the celebration. So probably was dancing, although only the upper torsos are visible because the lower part of the vase is missing. Hence, here too one cannot be completely sure that the celebrants' feet kept time together.

Such scenes are rare. For most of recorded history, portrayal of ordinary village dances in which rude, unskilled men, women, and children took part, did not attract the attention of artists working in durable, expensive materials. Those who danced could not pay artists' fees, and those who could thought such festivals unworthy of attention. Only when urbanism became so far removed from village life that prospering city dwellers could afford to yearn for the rural simplicity they had left behind, did skilled painters take up such themes. A half-page painting of a peasant dance in a prayer book from the fifteenth century offers the earliest example I have seen of this sort of idyllic visualization of rural reality.[6] In the next century, Pieter Brueghel's (d. 1569) paintings of peasant dancers supplied the same market. As far as I am aware, it is the first time that a famous artist bothered to record such thoroughly vulgar, utterly commonplace scenes for the delectation of rich and noble patrons.

Art, therefore, like literature, can tell us little about the history of community-wide dancing, even if the figures of the Trois Frères cave suggest that dancers (perhaps already professionalized) existed in Paleolithic times. But the Magdalenian artist who painted The Sorcerer lived perhaps 150,000 years after *Homo sapiens* first evolved in Africa, and something like 25,000 years after human bands had started to invent new tool types as never before. With a wide variety of bone, horn, and stone tools at their command, together with their famous cave paintings, the Magdalenians in fact represented a climactic flowering of Old Stone Age culture in Europe some eighteen to twelve thousand years ago.

Long before the Magdalenians created their cave paintings, language presumably guided human interaction with the external world, and did so more and more precisely and more and more comprehensively as the millennia passed. Gains in precision of cooperation, skill of execution, and adaptability to new circumstances were enormous. Language soon overshadowed clumsier and less flexible modes of gestural communication, but without extinguishing them or depriving gestures of their earlier communicative significance. Indeed, words and gestures still remain closely connected in ordinary human discourse, so much so that if words are not accompanied by the expected conventional facial and bodily motions, the emotional meaning of verbal communication is seriously impaired.[7]

If dancing was already part of the repertoire of human behavior when language emerged, then words had to interpret and give meaning to the feelings aroused by keeping together in time, and to any or all of the details of muscular movement involved on ritual occasions. We may surmise that such a deployment of words had the effect of elaborating and diversifying dance behavior. By attaching symbolic significance to particular dance occasions, ceremonies could be differentiated from one another, each marked by its appropriate dress, songs, specific movements, duration, and setting. Accordingly, initiation dances, war dances, wedding dances, harvest dances, and an indefinite number of other dance ceremonies could and did develop differently in different communities.

As dances acquired new, specific meanings in this fashion, different styles of dancing, like different types of tools, presumably began to evolve with unparalleled rapidity. Surviving stones and bones tell us of a burst of inventiveness in tool making. It is reasonable to assume that language provoked similar creativity and variability in other sorts of human behavior, including dancing. All the variations of dress, music, meaning, and muscular movement that characterize contemporary dancing in all the different societies of the earth were the result. Multiplicity reigns. General principles are hard to discover, and writers on dance history tend to conform to the pattern of their sources by concentrating on exhibitions of professional skill as developed first in religious, then in courtly, and later in theatrical circles.[8]

Professional dancers did indeed contribute to the rise of civilized complexity, as we shall soon see; but long before the earliest cities appeared on the face of the earth, and before written records allow even a glimpse of the meanings people attached to their activities, it is plausible to believe that the coexistence of language and dance, beginning some 40,000 years ago, had three general consequences for human society, each of which significantly expanded the basic and original function of reinforcing group feeling among the performers—a function presumptively inherited from *Homo erectus*.

First of all, important new meanings were attached to the extreme trance state that dancing can induce. This, indeed, became one of the important growth points for the enormously influential complex of rituals and beliefs that we call religion. Second, new forms of work became easier to endure and were performed more efficiently when people learned to labor together, moving their muscles rhythmically, and coordinating their action by song. Third, dancing became an efficacious way of consolidating distinct subgroups within larger communities, thus helping to prepare the way for the emergence of the comparatively vast and complex civilized societies familiar to us. These themes deserve to be explored a little further.

*Trance and religion.* Ordinary onlookers are bound to be puzzled by the onset of trance after prolonged, strenuous exertion; and, in the absence of firmly established expectations, those who experience such an altered state of consciousness also find it impossible to explain what took place.[9] Physiologists do not know exactly what happens when a dancer loses (or changes) consciousness. Perhaps the para-sympathetic nervous system asserts itself to check over-excitement arising from prolonged rhythmic stimulation; perhaps endorphins and other chemicals enter the bloodstream and modify or extinguish ordinary consciousness. Very likely both are involved, along with the sympathetic nervous system and all the different parts of the brain.

The trance-dance phenomenon, as observed in different contexts in recent times, seems very much influenced by social settings and expectation. Sometimes those in trance continue to dance and speak more or less intelligibly; sometimes they speak in tongues, unintelligibly; sometimes they return to ordinary consciousness with rich narrative details of their trance experience; sometimes they remember nothing. But in all cases, conspicuous changes in outward behavior make trance obvious and uncanny for onlookers when it occurs.[10]

Deep trance resembles sleep; and one modern observer has suggested that cataleptic trance is like the REM sleep we experience each night—both being neurological processes that restore or maintain a normal state of wakeful consciousness after a period of usual (or, for trance, unusual) wear and tear.[11] Sleep, of course, brings dreams that sometimes leave a disturbing emotional residue when the sleeper wakes. More particularly, dreamers sometimes encounter persons long dead or absent and may even converse with them. The same is sometimes reported by those who have recovered from trance. Deep trance and sleep also resemble death, with the difference that death is not followed by return to normal consciousness.

One of the results of acquiring language was that human beings could begin to foresee approaching death and wonder about its resemblance to sleep and trance.[12] The upshot of such wondering was that our remote ancestors hit upon the idea of a vital spirit, that was invisible (perhaps identical with the breath?) and separable from the body. When the spirit departed, sleep, trance, or death ensued. When it returned, ordinary life and consciousness resumed. This was and remains a very powerful notion. In all probability it was the first general idea capable of explaining so wide a spectrum of emotionally charged concerns affecting every human life. When it first dawned is impossible to say, but the fact that animism—to give the idea a modern label—is familiar among all peoples despite the enormous variety of their cultures implies that the notion arose very early, and perhaps before *Homo sapiens* dispersed across the face of the earth.

Once the idea that an invisible spirit inhabits each living human body had become well established, it followed that, on leaving its body behind in a state of trance, sleep, or death, a spirit might meet other disembodied spirits in its wanderings. Dream encounters with the dead proved that this did indeed occur. It followed that disembodied spirits constituted a world of their own, parallel to everyday life and obviously capable of influencing it, inasmuch as the spirits could and did move back and forth between the two worlds.

A further corollary of this world view was that spirits returning from encounters in the spirit world might carry important messages to the living. From such a point of view, dreams and whatever could be recollected from trance states became matters of special significance. Troubled individuals might even initiate communication with the spirits by deliberately inducing trance and dreams, and thus discover answers to all sorts of urgent questions. Over time the effort to enter into two-way communication with the spirit world provoked enormous elaboration of rites and ceremonies, constituting one of the principal growth points for religions in all their varieties.

A final corollary of belief in a world of spirits was the notion of possession. An evil spirit might, for reasons of its own, enter someone's body and produce physical and other ills. This was (and still is) a persuasive explanation of any and every sort of sickness—mental as well as physical. Moreover, whenever the normal, everyday spirit departed, a great variety of other spirits might also be supposed to take up temporary residence in a given person's body, thus explaining trances that result in sudden changes of styles of personal behavior.[13]

Taking all that we can plausibly surmise into account, the discovery (or invention) of invisible spirits, and the subsequent mapping of the spirit world that our remote ancestors engaged in, ought to be counted as one of the greatest intellectual accomplishments of our species. It was certainly the most enduring. Many millions of persons living today continue to believe in the existence of spirits that may wantonly invade a healthy body and cause pain and suffering; and thousands of professional exorcists continue to relieve their symptoms by conducting appropriate rituals. In modern cities, especially in the Third World and among the poor, innumerable ecstatic religious groups rely on song and dance to provoke trance, which is universally interpreted as an encounter with the spiritual world. And even thoroughly skeptical persons habitually describe unusual behavior—as in the phrase "an inspired performance"—by using words that imply the phenomenon of spiritual possession simply because it was taken for granted by Europeans and, I think, also by every other people of the earth, as recently as the seventeenth century.

No other way of interpreting the world has lasted nearly so long or met human needs so successfully in so many different cultural contexts. It therefore deserves serious respect as the most powerful and flexible world view ever invented.

A side-effect of this idea system was that trance-dance acquired a new social role by becoming the most reliable way of communicating with the spirit world. Dreams were difficult to orchestrate, though we know of attempts to institutionalize dreaming by sleeping in specially sacred spots after appropriate rituals so as to induce the desired spiritual encounter. In ancient Greece, for instance, persons suffering from serious illness commonly resorted to temples of Asclepius, where they hoped to encounter the god while asleep and learn from him how to regain their health. Sometimes such procedures produced expected results, but they often failed. But trance was far more predictable. Appropriate exercises regularly induced that state of consciousness, and, when primed with appropriate expectations, persons recovering from trance nearly always carried meaningful messages from the spirit world.

Some individuals were (and are) more liable to trance than others. Suitably susceptible dancers could thus become specialists in dealing with the spirits. How early this differentiation happened is impossible to say, but it may well date back to Paleolithic times. At any rate, shamanism, as it survives among pastoral and hunting peoples of northern Asia, is commonly supposed to descend from Paleolithic religious practices. This seems plausible, inasmuch as ideas and rituals that resemble Asian shamanism are widespread among hunters and gatherers in other parts of the earth.

Contemporary shamans enjoy a privileged status in the Asian societies where they exercise their art. Moving about in the spirit world is dangerous work, after all, for who knows what evil spirit they might encounter? As professionals, they expect fees for curing the sick and transmitting messages from the spirits that tell ordinary people what to do in particular situations. Details of ritual differ, but always involve drumming, rhythmic movement, and entry into trance by the shaman. Performances require active support from a circle of observers. A Russian anthropologist described shamanistic rites among the Tungus of northern Siberia as follows: "Rhythmic music and singing and later the dancing of the shaman gradually involve every participant," producing "deep satisfaction . . . because in shamanizing, the audience at the same time acts and participates."[14] Since such ceremonies usually take place inside a tent, only a few can be present; but their collective response to rhythmic sound and muscular movement helps to bring on the shaman's trance and prepares the participants for reception of the messages he brings back from the spirit world.[15]

Something resembling modern Tungus rites may have existed among Paleolithic hunters. Perhaps the Sorcerer of Trois Frères was ancestral to modern shamans, using dance and trance to communicate with spirits of the animals upon whose flesh the Magdalenians fed; but this sort of speculation about Paleolithic religious practices is unnecessary here. I intend only to argue that when words became available to explain and give meaning to the experience of dance-induced trance, dancing took on a new role in human society and became a prominent feature of many different religious systems,[16] beginning, very probably, with ancient forms of shamanism.

Dance and dance-like behavior continue to play a very prominent role in religion, whether or not trance states are involved. The emotional impact on human societies of keeping together in time at religious ceremonies was, indeed, second in general importance only to community-wide dancing at festivals; and, of course, the two regularly merged. Religious meanings often suffused festival celebrations, and religious ceremonies (with attendant dancing) frequently involved the whole community. The enrichment of meanings and elaboration of practices which such blending allowed became very prominent indeed in most human lives, from the time the idea of a spirit world was first adumbrated until our own time.

But in proportion as words explained and directed what needed to be done, the merely muscular and visceral levels of interaction created by dance, processionals, and other ritual movement, together with the emotional bonds they created and sustained, faded from consciousness. Trance was different, being too uncanny to escape continued notice. But it was also exceptional. Emotional residues from routinized religious exercises mattered more in most communities, and since emotion always affected human action, and in dubious situations could make the difference between success and failure, the rhythmic, muscular aspect of religious ritual retained far greater importance than written records reveal. The reason is simple. Knowing what was right and good and necessary (as set forth in words) was needed to sustain common action; and such convictions gained additional weight and force from the emotional residues of keeping together in time. As a result, those who danced together cooperated more wholeheartedly and therefore lived better and survived longer. The prevalence of dancing in civil society and of dance and dance-like behavior in religious ceremonies testifies to the real, practical advantages that flowed from keeping together in time.

*Work.* Among the practical advantages of keeping time with others was that it also relieved the tedium of repetitive tasks. This constituted a second path for the elaboration of dance-like behavior that found widening application as human populations shifted from hunting and gathering to food production. Processing of gathered food had always required some tedious effort—shelling nuts and soaking poisons from roots, or the like. But deliberate food production on a scale sufficient to tide a community over the winter months multiplied repetitive tasks enormously. Preparing ground for seed, planting, weeding, and harvest all involved long hours of dull, repetitive labor. Other jobs connected with food preparation were just as tedious: thrashing the grain, grinding it, kneading bread or shredding cassava, not to mention pressing grapes for wine and olives for oil. When groups shared these tasks, it was often possible for workers to exert their muscles in unison to the rhythm of song. Those who did so got more done in less time and felt better doing it, thus increasing the production of food and making the laboriousness of village life more bearable.

It seems likely that this was no small matter when food production was new. Human habits and aptitudes had been attuned from immemorial antiquity to the roving life of hunters and gatherers. In all probability ancient hunters enjoyed considerable leisure, and modern anthropologists have noted that contemporary hunters and gatherers do not usually work as long and hard as farmers commonly do. Agriculture required far more persistent effort with less immediate pay off.[17] It must have been hard to learn to bear the hours of muscular effort required to clear forested land, and to endure the back-breaking effort of eradicating weeds while preserving the crop. And this was only preliminary to the intense effort of harvesting grain in the few days when it was ripe but had not become so brittle that the ears would shatter as the harvester's sickle struck the stem, scattering precious seed on the ground. Thrashing, too, required prolonged effort to separate grain from straw and chaff, and the task of grinding grain into flour and then kneeding and baking bread ran uninterruptedly throughout the year. All of these tasks could be lightened by working together and keeping time to a rhythm established by song.

How universal such behavior may have been is impossible to say, but ethnographers of the nineteenth century observed rhythmic field work in many parts of the earth. In Bavaria, for instance, three to six men joined together to thrash grain, and village tradition held that six was the proper number because then the rhythm for swinging the flails attained an optimum pace that could be maintained all day long. In Polynesia women sang and moved in unison while shredding and pressing cassava roots to extrude their natural poisons. And in Madagascar a Frenchman reported seeing women planting upland rice by forming in line across the prepared field, bending to place a single seed in the ground and then stamping it into the earth, thus moving forward rhythmically "like a troop of dancers."[18]

Shared field work implied agreement about how to divide the harvest afterwards; and wherever separate families owned fields separately, the effects of working together rhythmically were correspondingly restricted to a smaller family circle which might, however, include hired hands for the harvest and other particularly urgent tasks. On the other hand, where plantation agriculture prevailed, gang labor in the fields could take full advantage of the improved efficiency that keeping together in time assured.

Slave work gangs in the United States, for instance, hoed cotton by keeping up with a "lead hoe"; he defined the pace at

which each worker moved along the row assigned to him or
her, while responding to the voice of a lead singer who set the
rhythm for everyone's muscular exertions. It is easy to under-
stand how this pattern of work produced better results than
anything that isolated individuals could or would have done.
The efficiency of slave labor in American agriculture, demonstrated by Robert W. Fogel and Stanley L. Engerman in their
famous book, *Time on the Cross: The Economics of American
Negro Slavery,*[19] presumably arose in good part from the way
rhythmic exertion in the fields made work more efficient. Yet
American slaves also sometimes used song and dance to express their alienation from whites by mimicking and mocking
their masters' behavior on festive occasions.[20]

Ancient civilizations of Eurasia relied on slave and other
forms of compulsory labor to accomplish many tasks that
single individuals and small family groups could not achieve by
working separately. For example, the irrigation systems upon
which ancient Mesopotamia and Egypt depended required
endless digging and diking; and water had sometimes to be
lifted from one level to another by human effort, using coun-
terweighted buckets or some other mechanical device. In nine-
teenth-century Egypt this sort of work was done rhythmically
by work teams,[21] and the practice is probably as old as irrigation itself. Monumental building, too, required gangs to shape
and move heavy stones into position, using levers, ropes, and
rollers. This was how the pyramids were built, as well as
Stonehenge and innumerable other ancient monuments.
Rhythmic pulling and heaving produced results otherwise un-
attainable. Iron metallurgy, similarly, required prolonged ham-
mering to shape tools and weapons; and when strong blows
were needed, smiths formed teams whose members took turns
swinging heavy hammers, thus creating a rhythm for their
work that sustained the effort beyond what could otherwise be
borne. Weavers did the same when using wide looms whose
shuttles moved beyond the reach of a single person.

Another domain in which rhythmic collective effort found much scope was navigation. Rowing and paddling were obviously rhythmic. Gangs pulling barges on canals and placid rivers in China and Russia coordinated their effort by song. The same was true of navigation on the high seas, where sea chanties timed the muscular effort required for lifting sails and anchors as well as for loading and unloading heavy cargo with block and tackle. Steam power took over these functions in the latter part of the nineteenth century, but the initial onset of steam also had the effect of opening a new, if transient, niche for rhythmic gang labor in the form of railroad construction. The importance of keeping together in time for building railroads is shown by the slang expression "gandy dancers," applied to the work gangs that laid rails across the American continent in the second half of the nineteenth century. For the phrase refers to the rhythmic motions with which such gangs tamped railroad ties into place and performed other heavy tasks that required cooperative muscular effort.

Taking things all in all, it seems safe to assert that keeping together in time while doing repetitive work pervaded much of human life, starting with the development of agriculture. Recently, machines replaced humans in many, perhaps in most, such situations in our cities, but rural populations of Asia, Africa, and Latin America still perform many age-old tasks in traditional ways.

From the point of view of the performers, repetitive work became far easier to bear when done together rhythmically, simply by virtue of the neurological and emotional responses to rhythmical movement that are built into human nervous systems. From the point of view of organizers, more got done in less time. In 1901, for instance, an American peach grower found that when he paid singers to keep time for women hired to pack peaches, they "remained fresher" and "on average 30 percent more peaches got packed"—thus more than paying for the cost of the music.[22] A German claimed in 1835 that "attentive rhythmic effort in a great variety of trades upped productivity by 25 percent," citing construction, weaving, mining, glass making, and tobacco processing as instances.[23]

If these estimates are anywhere near the mark, rhythmic labor obviously increased wealth substantially. More productivity improved living standards—sometimes for those who did the work, sometimes for those who organized it. In addition, keeping together in time permitted human muscles to do things that were otherwise beyond human capability, as the pyramids of ancient Egypt and the clipper ships and railroads of the nineteenth century attest.

*Consolidation of subgroups.* An important feature of emotional bonding through rhythmic muscular movement is that it affects those who take part in it more or less independently of how they may have been connected (or divided) by prior experience. Hence dance could and did become a way in which all sorts of new groups could define themselves, both by differentiation from within existing communities and by allowing marginalized persons or complete outsiders to coalesce into new, more or less coherent groups. All that was needed to achieve this end was to exclude some persons while admitting others to the dance.

Once again, no one knows when such practices began. They may conceivably antedate *Homo sapiens.* As we saw, sexual division of labor between male hunters and female gatherers probably developed among *Homo erectus* bands. As a result, males and females may have begun to dance separately—at least sometimes. But origins do not really matter. War and hunting dances did eventually bond adult males together, separating them from females and from mere boys. Likewise, age and gender differences eventually became status indicators, and rites to mark transition from one status to another became common. Initiation rites usually required youths to withdraw from everyday activity for a while and undergo special instruction and testing. Such ceremonies sometimes centered around symbolic death and rebirth, and were often secret. Males consorted with males, females with females, with different rituals prescribed for the two sexes. Almost always the initiates danced together, but variation was enormous, so it is silly to generalize about the consequences of the various practices for society as a whole other than to say that when youthful initiates danced together, they aroused feelings of commonality which may nor may not have lasted in later life, depending on how successive age cohorts assumed adult roles.[24]

To judge from what anthropologists were able to observe among simple societies of recent times, other sorts of enduring subgroups may have existed from very early times, even in rather small communities. Totemic clans that define who may marry whom among Australian aborigines offer one example; so do secret societies of Melanesia that exerted various kinds of social control upon their members and on outsiders as well. Experts in dealing with the supernatural were probably the oldest of all specialized groups, distinguished from ordinary persons by secret knowledge and skills that were passed on from one generation to another by private instruction. Verbal understandings and traditions defined all such subgroups; often, but not always, dancing reserved for members only reinforced their corporate identities as well.

The most important of these subgroups for subsequent human history were the specialists in dealing with the supernatural. In due time, in a few locations where unusual agricultural productivity sustained exceptional concentrations of population, powerful priestly colleges arose; and since such groups presided over the invention of writing, we know rather more about them and their corporate affairs than we do about other subgroups in early civilized societies.

The earliest priestly colleges whose written records can be read by modern scholars lived in Sumer. These records show that Sumerian priests participated in temple rituals that combined professionalized song and dance with routinized prayer and sacrifice. Their privileged social status and collective identity rested on elaborate verbal understandings of what the temple rituals meant; but here again it is reasonable to suppose that the emotional residue of keeping together in time during ritual performances also helped to bond the priestly participants together.

Very early in Sumerian history, priests simplified the confusion of the spirit world by discerning seven great gods who ruled the natural world and met together in council once a year to decide what would happen in the next twelve months. Each god also ruled over a special domain: sky, storm, sun, moon, fresh water, salt water, and earth. The seven great gods, in turn, matched up with the seven movable lights of the firmament: sun, moon, Mercury, Venus, Mars, Jupiter, and Saturn; and the number seven also fitted almost exactly into the phases of the moon which defined the agricultural calendar. These coincidences were enormously impressive, as indicated by the subsequent spread of the seven day week to distant China by about 1400 B.C., and completely around the globe after 1500 A.D.

The Sumerian pantheon became a second vastly influential world view, clarifying older animism by bringing political and astronomical precision to the confused multiplicity of the spirits. It allowed priests to elaborate ways of influencing the spirit world by going directly to the top. Simply by building a temple and a cult statue for a powerful god to inhabit, sacrifices, and other forms of magnificent and luxurious service might persuade the deity to protect those who treated him or her so well. Sometimes the god might even grant individual prayers or warn the people of impending danger.

By superimposing a ruling hierarchy of great gods on the multiplicity of spirits, and elaborating ways to communicate with the divine rulers of the spiritual and material worlds, the priests of course confirmed and expanded their own control over Sumerian society as a whole. In effect, they centralized access to the spirit world at a time when centralized control over everyday human activity was also attaining hitherto unparalleled scale owing to the technical requirements of irrigation agriculture. Crops in Sumer depended on irrigation; large-scale irrigation required the construction and maintenance of canals and regulation of how the water was distributed to the fields. Engineering works to tame the irregular flow of the Tigris-Euphrates had to be planned by a few but could only be realized by the work of many thousands of laborers.

To make such feats possible, the scale of human society had to expand far beyond older limits. Villages with no more than a few hundred inhabitants no longer sufficed. And the rich harvests that could be garnered from suitably irrigated alluvial flood plains made it possible to feed the necessary numbers and even to reserve additional labor and materials for the construction of monumental temples in a dozen or more interconnected cities. Cooperation and coordination of effort according to plan were needed to achieve these goals. This was what Sumerian priests successfully contrived between 4000 and 3000 B.C.[25]

Ideas were more important than muscles in bringing about this transformation of human society. Temples became centers for large-scale redistribution of resources. Grain from the harvest, delivered to temple warehouses, sustained the specialists who served the god in different ways. Priests and subordinate temple attendants performed daily rites designed to please the god, keeping him or her fed, clothed, and entertained with all possible magnificence. Specially skilled artisans produced luxury goods for use in the temple services, and some of their products were exported by merchants who brought back precious commodities from afar. Before long, military specialists were also needed to protect the wealth thus created in the Tigris-Euphrates flood plain. And, of course, burgeoning specialists were all sustained by toilers in the fields who produced the food they ate, parting with part of their harvest every year in return, presumably, for the divine protection that temple rituals were designed to assure.

As the number of persons engaged in these transactions grew, tallies were needed to supplement human memory. The effort to keep accurate record of who owed what to whom eventually led to the invention of cuneiform symbols that could record human speech fully. After that, one might expect that history based on written records might take over from the hazy speculation that has hitherto dominated these pages. But, alas, when one inquires into the social effects of keeping together in time, the written record does not help very much.

Very probably the occupational, ethnic, and other subgroups that combined to form Sumerian (and other subsequent) cities and civilizations danced together among themselves on appropriate occasions. But, like village dancing, this sort of behavior was too commonplace to be recorded. Surviving texts only imply, without describing in detail, the routines of temple ceremonies that involved professional song and dance.

We do know that on special occasions, notably the inauguration of the New Year when, it was believed, the high gods met to determine fate for the coming twelve months, priests and other temple attendants emerged from the closed interior of the temple for outdoor ceremonies where ordinary persons might watch them. Such rituals presumably helped to unite the city as a whole, reinforcing shared meanings through shared spectacle.

But so far as one can tell, with the rise of cities community-wide dancing and other ceremonies in which everyone took active part withered away. More intense commonality had to be reserved for subgroups, among which priests and other temple attendants on the one hand, and soldiers on the other, soon became the most influential. Indeed, differentiation of specialized subgroups was probably the most important feature of the emergence of civilized society, and despite the absence of written evidence, I feel sure that dancing played a part in bringing this to pass.

Another feature of civilized conditions of life was that marginalized persons multiplied. They came from different sources. In crowded landscapes, for example, rural youths sometimes found it difficult or impossible to gain access to land and take on normal adult roles. In cities, drifters and strangers frequently found it hard to make a living. And peoples at the geographical margins of civilized society often found their inherited ways of life crumbling away into futility as a result of collision with the superior knowledge, skills, and power of distant rulers and oppressors.

Such desperate and disappointed persons often responded to unhappy circumstances by inventing new communities for themselves. Such communities were tied together partly by ideas about future redress of grievances (often by supernatural agency), and partly by practical mutual support. And, as innumerable such groups discovered, at the practical level, keeping together in time was the most efficacious way to establish warm emotional bonds among marginalized and distressed persons of any and every sort.

As a result, rhythmic movement in religious ritual and military display that confirmed and sustained constituted authority came to be countered by dance and song among the dispossessed, thereby creating a counterculture that was consciously at odds with the world of the rich and powerful in one degree or another. Such differences led to distrust, but outright hostility was an extreme that seldom lasted long.

Instead, various compromises between the haves and have-nots were hit upon. One pattern, exemplified by the Roman Saturnalia and modern Carnival celebrations, allowed the poor to pretend to change places with the rich and powerful for a few days of the year. Another, illustrated by the Hebrew prophets, was to accord semi-sacred status to specially designated spokesmen for the dispossessed, even (or especially) when they denounced prevailing injustices. Sometimes countercultures cowered in secret, as was true of some early Christian communities. Sometimes such groups withdrew into remote fastnesses, as Jim Jones's followers did before committing mass suicide in 1978. And occasionally, discontent boiled over into armed revolt, as innumerable peasant and other rebellions illustrate.

Dance and song played a part in most, perhaps in all, such dissident communities, but details varied from case to case and were very imperfectly recorded. Only extreme and unusual conduct was likely to attract conscious attention and enter written records. This tends to exaggerate ecstatic dance-trance behavior at the expense of more commonplace dancing and singing.

The earliest recorded example of ecstatic countercultural behavior dates from the eighteenth century B.C., when persons who went by a special name—appropriately translated as prophet—appeared in Syria. They were, or claimed to be, inspired, and a few surviving texts record the blunt, peremptory advice they gave to the king of Mari. That is all that is known about them.[26] Exactly what they did to invite inspiration can only be guessed. Analogy with Biblical passages, describing how the false "prophets of Baal" invited their god's presence among them by dancing, singing, and cutting themselves with knives, makes it almost certain that keeping together in time was part of prophetic behavior.[27]

By attacking the wickedness of the rich and powerful, prophets helped to shape historic Judaism. And with the appearance of the so-called higher religions, innumerable sects, operating in more or less explicit opposition to the wickedness of surrounding society, became widespread beginning in the first millennium B.C. Buddhist communities in China and Japan had a particularly vivacious and shadowy history. Christians, Jews, and Moslems also formed innumerable sects and circles of protest. Similar groups continue to flourish in the slums of contemporary cities, combining dance and song with preaching against prevailing wickedness. I will return to these religious phenomena in the next chapter, but wish here to turn attention to a few scattered examples of how more nearly secular dancing can heal, or try to heal, human distress by helping to form new *ad hoc* communities.

Dance manias that broke out in medieval Europe in times of unusual hardship, beginning as early as 1278 and cresting in the wake of the Black Death (1346–1350), offer one example. On these occasions, crowds of distressed people gathered together in public places and danced for hours on end, sometimes collapsing in exhaustion, sometimes attaining trance, and always achieving a general catharsis. Upper-class observers were amazed and sometimes alarmed. A subsequent interpretation was to suppose that these outbreaks of frenetic dancing were manifestations of a strange new disease. Paracelsus (d. 1541), an innovative medical practitioner, was the first to express this view; and medical writers of the nineteenth century concurred. In some cases ergot poisoning from eating infected rye may have played a part in provoking convulsions. But it is more plausible to suppose that the release of anxiety that mass dancing provoked was the main factor sustaining these outbreaks.

Eventually, public authorities in Venice and other towns of Europe that were especially exposed to return visits of bubonic plague channeled public anxiety into elaborate civic rituals, featuring solemn processionals through the streets and invoking protection from St. Sebastian. Unorganized, spontaneous outbreaks of popular dancing as a response to plague correspondingly decayed, though in ill-governed parts of southern Italy a frenetic popular form of dance, the Tarantella—explained, however, as being the result of spider bites—became semi-institutionalized and persisted into the nineteenth century.[28]

After 1789, some secularized Frenchmen, in revolt against traditional religion, also found dance useful for asserting their new-found fraternity. During the Revolution itself a sudden vogue for a dance known as the Carmagnole became an informal way of affirming participants' dedication to revolutionary principles, while "Liberty trees" sprouted in public places for more formal, official demonstrations of the same sentiments. Such trees had figured also in the American Revolution. Around them men and women were expected to dance in a circle, thus enacting "a joining of hands of different ranks and orders in the fraternal unity established by the new order."[29] When revolutionary ardor was at its height in 1793, large numbers of persons did so with some enthusiasm. Planners in Paris were acutely aware of the power of dance. Their intent, on the words of a modern scholar, was clear. "July 14 was a dance, a masterpiece of pure activity in which the movements of a unanimous people were miraculously ordered in the figure of a gracious, gratuitous ballet."[30]

But revolutionary festivals did not take any real root in France, partly because the leadership in Paris was unstable and each new regime revised official instructions about what should be celebrated, and partly because peasants clung to Christian and even to pre-Christian rituals, resisting governmental fiat even when ostensibly obeying. They were, for example, fully capable of reading different meanings into dances around Liberty trees than the members of the Convention in Paris intended, and probably did so even when revolutionary enthusiasm was at its height.[31]

Subsequently, when revolutionary principles were under a cloud, a few restless young men inspired by the teachings of Henri de Saint Simon (d. 1825) formed a sect designed to transform France through the power of their ideas and the example of their community life. Dancing together and sporadic outbreaks of trance expressed the intensity of their efforts to replace traditional bonds of family, religion, and locality with scientific, secular, and socialist truth.[32] In the 1960s and 1970s some of the hippie communities in the United States did much the same.

An interesting recent example of how keeping together in time can create group solidarity among marginalized individuals is offered by the history of the Beni in Tanganyika. Beginning about 1890 young men in coastal cities formed into rival teams, mimicking European military drill and accompanying their performances with songs that commented, sometimes derisively, on current events. Beni teams built upon older traditions of competitive dancing whereby kinship and other groups had been accustomed to exhibit their prowess in public performances. But Beni dancers accepted persons from diverse kindreds and backgrounds into their ranks, and, as they developed a distinct *esprit de corps,* took on various forms of mutual aid—providing a proper funeral for deceased members, settling disputes among the living, and, through their public performances, making all concerned feel better about the confusing new experiences that living under European colonial administration involved. During World War I Beni dance groups spread inland; and when the British supplanted German colonial administration, they divided into rival Scottish and English drill teams, mimicking and sometimes mocking British military rituals.

Within Tanganyikan society the members of Beni dance teams were modernizers, affected by European influence and alienated, in greater or lesser degree, from traditional social ties. Their relation to the colonial authorities was, however, ambiguous: part admiration, part challenge. In the 1930s British administrators decided that Beni dancers constituted a potential threat to their authority, and discouraged public performances. Under the pressure of official distrust, the organizations gradually faded away, and disappeared entirely by 1960.[33] Other dance groups have since come to the fore, both religious and secular. Indeed, political meetings and crowds of every kind in Tanzania and other African states regularly resort to dance as a way of expressing and sustaining public excitement. But so far as I know, none have so clearly played the role of bringing marginalized individuals together by forming exotic new groups in the way the Beni dance teams did.

The tension between old and new ways of life that Beni dancers sought to overcome in Tanganyika was a weaker instance of the wholesale distresses that afflict small societies when traditional ways break down as a result of collision with powerful outsiders. The usual response to such crises is religious. Efforts to enlist supernatural aid to restore justice and righteousness have taken innumerable forms.[34] Two well-known instances are the sudden rise of the Ghost Dance religion among American Indians in the late nineteenth century, and the more recent vogue of the so-called Cargo cult in Melanesia. Each deserves brief description.

Indian "prophets" in North America, who preached reform and promised some sort of return to conditions of life before the arrival of white men, date back at least to 1762; and a few of them met with partial practical success.[35] The Ghost Dance, however, ended in disaster. It started when millennial hope of restoring a vanished past spread like wildfire among several Indian peoples, beginning in 1889, when a Paiute Indian named Wovoka had a vision in which God gave instructions for moral and ritual reform and promised earthly renewal for those who obeyed the new revelation. Wovoka had encountered Presbyterians, Mormons, and Shakers before having this vision, and some motifs of his teaching derived from these sources. But Wovoka also taught that long dead ancestors—together with the buffalo they had lived on—would return, and white men would disappear, if everyone followed the new prescriptions for reform.

Dancing that often lasted until the participants dropped from exhaustion was the most conspicuous outward sign of the movement. When the hope and excitement it provoked flared up among the warlike Sioux nation, white men were alarmed. Resulting distrust and fear soon provoked a detachment of the U.S. Cavalry to massacre a fleeing party of Sioux at Wounded Knee in 1890. This halted the movement in its tracks; but the circumstances of the slaughter were sufficienly shocking at the

time to provoke systematic inquiry into the Ghost Dance religion and its connection with what turned out to be the last
battle between white men and Indians in North America. To
this we owe surprisingly exact knowledge of how the religion
arose, spread, and collapsed.[36]

The Cargo cult of Melanesia had a more complicated history
and is less well recorded. Manifestations began as early as
1885 and became especially exuberant between 1930 and
about 1950. As was true of the Ghost Dance religion, Christian
millenarian ideas helped to stimulate self-chosen preachers to
announce that a new era would shortly begin, when ancestors
would return from the dead bringing a cargo of all sorts of
exotic and precious goods with them. Upon their return wage
work on European-managed plantations would end, and,
Melanesians would be supplied with all the foreign goods they
wanted in the same mysterious way that ships (and later, in
World War II, airplanes) brought such goods to their European
employers and administrators.

Old ways had obviously came under strain when colonial
authorities began to fold the Melanesian islands into a global
system of commerce by fostering copra production for export;
and the Cargo cult seized upon particularly dramatic aspects
of that engagement with the outside world by combining expectation of a cargo of new and exotic foreign goods with
ancestral return. Collapse of traditional Melanesian society
was not as profound as that suffered by the Sioux and other
Plains Indians when the buffalo disappeared, since slash-and-
burn agriculture remained the basis of ordinary subsistence as
before. But the seemingly miraculous way in which Europeans
could summon material goods from afar was profoundly disturbing. "Why do such gifts not come to us too?" was a
question traditional religion and custom could not answer.
Hence the invention of Cargo cults, and their surreptitious
propagation from one discontented community to another.

What resident Europeans noticed was that whenever and

wherever the Cargo cult took hold, their employees quit work to engage in dances, marches, and other activities (for example, construction of landing places for ships or airplanes) that were expected to bring the ancestors back along with everything new that the heart might desire. Such events occurred sporadically, now in one place, now in another, and always wore themselves out after varying periods of time. Dancing could not last forever, and expectations could not be maintained indefinitely when the expected cargo failed to show up. Moreover, colonial authorities often sought to break what looked to them more like a strike than a religious revelation by arresting ring leaders. The Cargo cult therefore attained only brief overt expression, though some sort of underground hope clearly connected successive outbursts, until after World War II it changed into overtly political agitation for independence—a movement that achieved success in 1973 when Papua New Guinea became a sovereign state.[37]

Thus the Ghost Dance and the Cargo cults were evanescent efforts to restore wounded societies. The prominent role that dancing played in both movements shows how keeping together in time can excite sentiments of hope and solidarity among distressed peoples when old ways are in serious disarray. Rallying to lost causes, by definition, never played a very large role in human history, but it is worth noting as yet another example of how emotions aroused by dancing express and sustain collective human actions—even those destined to fail.

A final observation about dancing in small groups seems worth inserting at this point. The excitement aroused by rhythmic movement with others is inherently diffuse. Heightened emotion can find various and even contradictory expressions, depending on the expectations participants bring to the exercise. These, of course, are verbally defined, so that identical (or almost identical) motions of arms and legs may induce love or hate, exorcise danger, or invite possession by the spirits. Within the emotional spectrum aroused by dance, sexual exhibition and excitement are always latent and often become explicit. Since the Renaissance, this aspect of dancing has tended to displace others in European society, first in courtly circles and later in middle-class urban ballrooms, until in our own time mass culture has made song and dance almost synonymous with sex throughout the world. This constitutes a specialized, historically exceptional meaning, and has helped to blind us to the other roles that dancing played in other times and places.

A direct and obvious contradiction exists between emotional solidarities shared by all participants, and the pairing off that sexual excitement invites. In early human times this contradiction may have been critical, inasmuch as the practical advantages of consolidating larger communities through dance could not be achieved without minimizing linkages between dance and sexual pairing. How this may have been done is of course unknowable. I merely suggest that bands that were successful in cultivating community-wide performance, insulating emotions thus aroused from the mating game, had an important advantage over any groups that failed to consolidate fellow-feeling within the entire community by dancing together. If that was so, we can assume that community-wide dancing was in fact effectually separated from sexual pairing off in most or all early human communities. It follows that the direction dancing has taken in recent centuries in the western world is exceptional and may even be regarded as a social pathology, insofar as it preempts the conscious meanings we attach to keeping together in time and thereby inhibits the role of dance in consolidating entire communities.[38]

I CONCLUDE that the extraordinary variability of meanings that human beings can attach to the emotional arousal of dance (and less energetic forms of rhythmic movement like stately processionals and military drill) was fundamental in widening and differentiating social bonds among our species. Its primary manifestation was to strengthen and stabilize small, isolated communities where everyone took part in festival dances. Rhythmic exertion also faciliated the performance of dull, repetitive tasks and expanded what was possible for human muscles to achieve by coordinating the effort of gangs of laborers. And in complex, larger societies, public rituals involving rhythmic movement regularly helped to confirm constituted authorities, while an indefinite number of subgroups availed themselves of the emotional uplift of dancing together to define and strengthen their differing identities as well.

In all these ways, the practical efficiency and emotional residues of moving together in time influenced the human past in ways seldom noticed and very imperfectly recorded. Yet defects of surviving records ought not to prevent more careful, critical consideration of this dimension of human sociality if others choose to explore in greater detail what is here set forth in sketchy, preliminary form.

# Religious Ceremonies

As in human life at large, words define religious meanings. But public worship always involves muscular gestures and ritualized performances as well. Song and rhythmic movement are usual, varying from frenetic dance to solemn processional. Spontaneous outbreaks of inspired speech and gesture characterize enthusiastic groups, but such behavior requires interpretation to make it fit existing expectations, thus allowing private inspiration to acquire ongoing significance. Dance, music, and song are the most reliable way to generate inspiration; they also cement solidarity among participants. No wonder, therefore, that song and dance figure so largely in religious history, since from that spring came a perennial strengthening of group identities as well as perennial challenge and renewal, thanks to fresh encounters with the supernatural that always had to be reconciled with established practices derived from previous encounters.

The history of every major religion of the civilized world exhibits a resulting tension between formalized ritual routines and red-hot inspiration from below, variously annealed into the ongoing tradition, or splitting off into a new, rival, and related faith. The historic succession connecting Judaism with Christianity and Islam illustrates this pattern, as do the histories of innumerable sects within each of the three religions. Brahmanism, Buddhism, and Hinduism have a similar, though rather more amorphously interconnected history.

Not infrequently, techniques for inducing emotionally intense communion with the supernatural leaped across linguistic and religious boundaries. Thus Indian styles of asceticism infiltrated Christianity in the early Christian centuries; a similar upsurge of mysticism transformed Islam after about 1000, modeled partly on Indian and Christian examples of how to walk familiarly with God. In our own time, increased contact across religious traditions coincides with widespread disruption of traditional patterns of life—especially of rural village life. As a result, religious invention—always or nearly always expressed in dance and song as well as in words—has reached flood stage among the poor and dispossessed of the earth.

Let me, then, offer a few examples of how song and dance and resultant emotional bonding affected the history of religion and society, beginning with the dancing prophets of the Old Testament.

T HE RISE of the Hebrew monarchy was intimately connected with support from bands of prophets, who danced and sang to induce divine frenzy. Some sort of connection between prophecy in Mari, mentioned in the preceding chapter, and prophecy among the Hebrews is probable, but evidence is lacking. According to the Book of Kings, prophets of Baal—the Canaanites' god of storm and fertility—"leaped upon the altar" and "cut themselves with knives after their manner until the blood gushed out upon them"[1] as they implored their god to visit them and show his power. Similar vigorous muscular exertions prevailed among Hebrew prophets, who danced and sang to pipes, drums, and stringed instruments until, in a state of ecstasy, they prophesied.[2] Prophetic behavior sometimes violated ordinary restraints, as when Saul, having joined the prophets, "stripped off his clothes also, and lay down naked all that day and all that night."[3]

Everyone understood that prophets were inspired by God when frenzy seized them. This gave them an ambiguous status in society at large, for they were holy and close to God, yet remained outside ordinary society, being only marginally attached to places where sacrifices to Jahweh took place. Frenzy and trance were uncanny in themselves; and the God of Battles who inspired the prophets in the eleventh century B.C. was distinctly dangerous, being more often angry than loving.

The ambiguous role that bands of prophets played in Hebrew society lurks behind the story of how Saul prepared himself for kingship. Samuel, the Bible says, having privately recognized Saul as future king, told the young man that presently he would encounter a band of prophets "coming down from the high place with a psaltery, a tabret, and a pipe, and a harp before them: and they shall prophecy. And the Spirit of the Lord shall come upon thee and thou shalt prophecy with them, and shalt be turned into another man."[4] So indeed it turned out, to the dismay of at least some of his former associates, as the Bible story also makes clear, saying: "And it came to pass, when all that knew him beforetime saw that behold he prophesied among the prophets, then the people said one to another, What is this that has come unto the son of Kish? Is Saul also among the prophets?"[5] Subsequently, after his anointment as king, Saul collected a "band of men, whose hearts God had touched" who went home with him. Presumably they formed the core of the army he summoned to fight the Ammonites when, shortly afterwards, "the Spirit of the Lord came upon Saul" once again.[6]

These passages make it clear that Saul's military leadership was closely connected with ecstatic, collective prophecy. He and those who followed him into battle were inspired by God, thus sharing that special link with the God of Battles that the prophets of Jahweh enjoyed. Saul's monarchy also shared the social ambiguity of prophecy, for the Book of Samuel portrays

the upstart king both as divinely chosen to fight against enemies of God's people and also as a usurper of God's rightful
place as ruler of his chosen people.[7] Even his fits of inspiration
were ambiguous, for Saul was sometimes liable to seizure by
"an evil spirit from God," so that, on one fateful occasion, he
"prophesied in the midst of the house" before attacking David
with a javelin.[8] Separate manuscript traditions and subsequent
editorial emendations undoubtedly lie behind the contradictory tenor of these passages. But the narrative as passed down
to us surely reflects acute differences of opinion during Saul's
lifetime, when this violent, innovative leader began to create an
army and the tax system needed to support it.

David, whose independent military career initially attracted
"everyone that was in distress, and everyone that was in debt,
and everyone that was discontented,"[9] also associated with
prophets, and on occasion danced before the Lord with as
much abandon as Saul had been wont to do. Like Saul, he also
aroused disdain by ecstatic behavior.[10] But, building on precedents from Saul's time, David's monarchy quickly evolved into
a bureaucratic structure, with a professional soldiery (some of
them foreigners) supported by a corps of ruthless tax collectors. A few prophets came to court, where they maintained an
ambiguous relation with the king. The prophet Nathan, for
example, sanctified David's government by declaring that it
was God's will that "thine house and thy kingdom shall be
established forever";[11] but was also inspired to protest against
David's wickedness in arranging to have Uriah killed, and then
taking Uriah's wife, Bathsheba, into his harem.[12]

Other prophets maintained the old pattern of group life
around sanctuaries; still others became solitary holy men,
dwellers in the wilderness. This split between court prophets
and those who remained on the fringes of society symbolizes
the divergent roles the prophets played among the Hebrews.
First of all, they facilitated the rise of the monarchy and
confirmed its association with obedience to Jahweh, God of

Battles. Without the link between prophets of Jahweh and the first two kings of Israel, it is hard to believe that the encroachment of Baal worship—amply attested in subsequent reigns, beginning with the wise Solomon himself[13]—could have been successfully resisted. That eventual outcome, however, depended both on the political failure of the Hebrew kingdoms, and on the ambiguous status of court prophets, like Elijah and Elisha, whose inspiration required them to attack the court's religious syncretism by asserting the rightful exclusivity of Jahweh-worship. As a result, even the mightiest court prophets never entirely separated themselves from their marginalized fellows, since stern pronouncements in the name of Jahweh could and often did arouse royal anger, whereupon flight to the wilderness, where they joined the chorus of prophetic criticism of the high and mighty, became necessary—or at least prudent.

The principal religious growth point among the Hebrews turned out to be the work of humble, marginalized prophets who never got to the royal court, and instead reproached the rich and powerful by demanding justice and righteousness in the name of God. Across the generations, new ideas about how God wanted men to behave arose among them, and, beginning with Amos (ca. 720 B.C.), some of the prophets' pronouncements were recorded in writing and eventually entered the Jewish and Christian scriptures.[14]

The biblical account of the rise and fall of the Hebrew monarchy played an enormous role in defining Jewish and Christian ideas of proper forms of government in subsequent centuries. The prophetic demand for justice and true piety was even more influential. Prophetic ideas survived and spread only after the inspiration of prophecy, which had begun as a collective muscular-musical path to God, turned into solitary inspiration—a transmutation that conferred world-transforming power on a handful of literary prophets. Once written down, their private encounter with God escaped from the ordinary limits of time and place. Preserved in Sacred Scripture, their thoughts survive to the present as a living force among many millions of people.

It is indeed extraordinary to reflect upon how these marginalized (and probably young) men, bound together by shared response to song and dance and by the transitory experience of ecstasy, managed to leave such lasting monuments behind them. Without the prophets the Jewish, Christian, and Moslem religions would be inconceivable and the history of the world would be very different indeed. Yet the literary prophets were shaped by an older tradition of song and dance, for what gave prophecy its weight in Hebrew society in the time of Saul and David were the inward affects and outward manifestations of keeping together in time. By dancing together and thereby inducing ecstasy, small groups of men thus changed the course of human history in ways no one could have imagined at the time.

It seems to be almost as hard to recognize in retrospect, for scholarly writing about the Hebrew prophets pays scant, embarrassed attention to the frenzied, muscular, and collective aspect of their behavior and focuses instead on individual figures like Moses, Samuel, and Elijah before turning (with an almost audible sigh of relief?) to the ideas expressed by the literary prophets. Given the role of prophetic literature in the subsequent history of Judaism and Christianity, it is proper for modern scholars to take the words of the books of prophecy to heart; but this does not justify the way some of them deliberately avert their eyes from Saul's nakedness.[15] Yet never before or since, I venture to suggest, has so much depended on so few.

An analogous movement also affected the religion and culture of ancient Greece. At about the same time that Saul was consorting with bands of prophets in Israel, Dionysiac and Orphic worship spread around the shores of the Aegean. Their ceremonies also provoked ecstasy, thanks to the combined effect of music, dance, and wine.[16] Nothing so influential as the Hebrew monarchy or the prophetic definition of justice and piety emerged from these ritual occasions, but in due course the Dionysiac celebrations at Athens gave birth to public dramatic performances from which classical and modern theater descends. What began as ecstatic singing and dancing evolved into elaborate and eventually professional choral performances. The emotional impact on performers and audiences can only be guessed; but we can still admire the literary and intellectual vigor with which tragic dramatists of the classical age explored enduring moral and intellectual questions, and we may even enjoy the raucous social criticism that found expression in comedy.

Like biblical prophecy, the texts of a few of these dramas entered into the cultural heritage of modern Europe. Both descend from religious inspiration generated by keeping together in time. In both instances, moreover, it is worth pointing out that the supercession of muscular by literary inspiration recapitulated the way I believe that muscularly generated emotional bonding had been superseded by linguistic communication in the evolution of humanity. The verbal embodiment of both traditions was what mattered in later ages; without its ecstatic, muscular origin, however, prophetic and dramatic literature could not have taken the form they did. In this real but limited sense, therefore, it seems clear that classical drama belongs beside biblical prophecy as a second instance of how the inspiration of song and dance can sometimes echo across the centuries, long after the initial ecstasy has faded away.

By THE TIME Christianity emerged from its Jewish cradle, Scripture had displaced inspiration as the only officially recognized source of religious truth, and Jewish religious leaders cooperated closely with Jewish and Roman political authorities to keep inspiration from breaking out anew. That is why John the Baptist and Jesus were executed. But Jesus' most dedicated followers were not quieted. Instead, they discovered the Risen Christ and, by preaching his Second Coming, aroused intense hope and excitement among a small community of the faithful in Jerusalem. This provoked new frictions with the constituted political and religious authorities on the spot, but the community survived, and from this tiny seed all the historic Christian churches descend.

The first Christians were Jews who shared the overwhelming emphasis on God's word as set forth in Sacred Scripture, which distinguished Judaism from all other religions. And, in due course, they reaffirmed the primacy of the written Word over all other paths to God when they added the New Testament to the Old. Hence, despite some famous individual episodes like Paul's cataleptic conversion and Peter's trance,[17] congregational exercises promoting mystic encounter with God are scarcely mentioned in the New Testament. But words alone—preaching the Risen Christ, awaiting his Second Coming, and interpreting the events of Jesus' life on earth in the light of their messianic expectations—were enough to generate intense collective excitement, whose principal manifestation came to be "speaking with tongues." Breaking out suddenly at Pentecost,[18] "speaking with tongues" was interpreted as visitation by the Holy Spirit of God. Glossolalia, to use the technical term for this behavior, soon came to be accepted as proof of the authenticity of conversions to the new faith; and when Samaritans[19] and even a Roman centurion[20] also started to speak with tongues, old barriers between Jews and Gentiles came tumbling down within the expanding Christian community.

Modern sects that reverence speaking with tongues as a sign of divine inspiration invariably supplement preaching with music, song, and rhythmic bodily movements;[21] but these enhancements may not have entered Christian worship until the initial intensity of millenarian expectation began to cool. How and when song and dance began to strengthen shared emotions among the Christian communities of the Roman empire is unknown, but keeping together in time did, for a while, apparently play a considerable part in consolidating fellow-feeling among members of Christian churches.

Towards the end of the second century, according to one authority, "church dances appear to have become part of the divine service. At the close of prayers, hands were raised above the head to a brief tramping or stamping dance,"[22] signifying the hope of attaining Heaven, where by this time it was understood that departed Christian souls joined the angels in a perpetual dance around the throne of God.[23] St. Basil of Caesarea (d. 379), the author of an influential monastic rule, approved of imitating the dance of Heaven by dancing in circles on earth; and St. Ambrose of Milan (d. 397) believed that suitably holy dancing in church helped to carry souls to Heaven, since, in his own words, "He who dances in the spirit with a burning faith is carried aloft and is uplifted to the stars. . . . He who dances the spiritual dance, always moving in the ecstasy of the faith, acquires the right to dance in the ring of all Creation," that is, in Heaven.[24] These words surely suggest that Christians sometimes achieved ecstasy by dancing together in church. If so, the experience must have helped to create the vigor and cohesion that Christian congregations exhibited in the fourth and fifth centuries, when most of the pagan institutions of Roman society were crumbling away.

At the same time, Ambrose deplored lascivious dancing and some modern scholars hold that the "spiritual dance" he recommended took place entirely in the mind and lacked any sort of bodily expression.[25] Moreover, his younger contemporary, St. Augustine (d. 430), was so horrified by the sexual arousal connected with popular dancing that he could only express a grudging toleration of the holy dances that Ambrose had praised.[26] In time, Augustine's views prevailed. Busy ecclesiastical administrators feared popular excitement of every kind, and since congregational dancing did indeed excite warm and even ecstatic emotions, it fell under increasing suspicion when, after 312, Christianity ceased to be a persecuted sect and, before the end of the century, became the established religion of the Roman empire.

Christian monasticism opened another path to God for especially dedicated souls. From anarchic beginnings, it also came under hierarchical control when the monastic rules of St. Basil and St. Benedict (d. 547) became normative. The first monks who withdrew into the deserts of Egypt and Syria to commune with God were of course following the example of innumerable prophets. Some of them resorted to bodily disciplines that appear to have been modeled on those of itinerant holy men from India. A few of these "gymnosophists" circulated in Mediterranean lands during the early Christian centuries and impressed learned and simple alike by virtue of their conspicuous ability to enter into trance at will after appropriate bodily and mental preparation.[27] But Indian yoga and the ascetic practices of early Christian mystics were individual achievements, usually centering on sensory deprivation rather than on shared muscular exertion.[28] This minimized public engagement, making exceptional holiness into a spectacle that was only weakly shared with pious bystanders.

Even so, once the Christian church allied itself with imperial officials, the monks' unpredictable personal encounters with God troubled both lay and clerical dignitaries. Eventually, duly constituted authorities constrained nearly all Christian monks to live together in monasteries and conform to rules, thus ending public outbreaks of the sort that had occasionally turned Egyptian hermits into leaders of riotous crowds.[29] Congregational singing, processionals, and other stately forms of worship played a conspicuous part in the new monastic rules, supplanting most of the private, trance-inducing exercises that individual monks had formerly engaged in. This strengthened public and ecclesiastical order by damping back the unruly emotions associated with direct and personal encounter with God.

Ambivalence about the emotions aroused by intense mystical experience, and by the weaker but more widely shared responses to song and dance, persisted in ecclesiastical circles throughout the Middle Ages. Too much enthusiasm was always an embarrassment to constituted authority; and after the Emperor Theodosius (d. 395) made Athanasian Christianity the official religion of the Roman state, the privileged Christian clergy tended to standardize their chant and song, together with processionals and other ritual gestures, and discouraged congregational participation. Bishops ceased to lead sacred dances as once had been the case, if St. John Chrysostom (d. 389) is to be believed;[30] but sacred gestures, like crossing oneself, or bowing to the ground in prayer, were always approved, and professional choristers never supplanted congregational singing entirely.

Churchmen seldom accorded merely muscular manifestations of religious excitement the dignity of literary notice, so that a full history of dancing in Christian churches is impossible. By and large, however, it appears to be the case that the formal alliance between throne and altar, concluded in course of the fourth century, had the effect of gradually throttling enthusiastic forms of dance and song in Christian worship, and banished popular dancing to the churchyard and other public spaces. Thereafter, lingering associations with pagan festivals on the one hand, and the sexual overtones of some popular dances on the other, meant that Augustine's denunciations of licentiousness prevailed over the praise for holy and ecstatic dancing that Ambrose had expressed. Yet enthusiasm could not be always suppressed; and in Carolingian times, as drawings in the Utrecht Psalter attest, "for men as for angels, the praise of God transmuted itself into collective dancing"—at least occasionally.[31]

With the rise of towns after 1000 A.D. new modes of life put fresh strains on Christian Europe. In the West, papal efforts to regularize, reform, and centralize ecclesiastical administration had to cope with recurrent efforts at renewal from below. Inspiration often found overt muscular expression, as when St.

Francis danced with his followers in the pontiff's presence in 1209, after Pope Innocent III had informally endorsed the Franciscan effort to live in exact and literal imitation of Christ.[32] Similarly, in the next century, a Flemish mystic, Jan van Ruysbroeck (1293–1391), wrote of the celestial vision to which he aspired: "It makes one unstable in all members so that one must run and jump and dance."[33]

In the Orthodox East an emotionally powerful upsurge of monastic mysticism, known as hesychasm, actually took over the Patriarchate of Constantinople in the 1340s,[34] but in the Latin West most expressions of popular piety were kept within the bounds of obedience to the hierarchical church until the sixteenth century, when Luther and other Protestant reformers repudiated papal authority. The resulting religious upheaval was, of course, profound. True to tradition, quarrels over the meaning of Scripture and the exact wording of creeds dominated resulting controversy. Vigorous muscular expressions of religious emotion manifested themselves mainly among Anabaptists and other extreme groups, and then only for short periods of time.[35] Still, Luther and Calvin both approved of congregational singing along with the comparatively restrained muscular movements that accompanied song. As a result, Lutheran hymns and Calvinist psalmody became important aids in winning popular commitment to their respective creeds. On the other hand, revulsion against the popular excitement aroused by Anabaptists and other radical sects led the Protestant reformers to banish dancing and associated ecstatic muscular convulsions from church services more rigorously than ever before.

Accordingly, from the sixteenth century onwards decorous rituals prevailed in established churches of all denominations, and popular muscular participation in church services was reduced to well-defined conventional gestures, supplemented, among Protestants, by comparatively subdued, but nonetheless pervasive, rhythmic movements incidental to congregational singing. Eventually, the introduction of pews in western Europe, allowing people to sit through sermons, restrained spontaneous muscular responses to the most fiery of preachers, and, by isolating one person from another with wooden barriers, introduced a new quiescence into public worship.[36]

In Catholic Europe mystical piety and concomitant dancing continued to crop up occasionally, as when St. Teresa (d. 1582) danced before God in a chapel at Avila, keeping time with her own tambourine.[37] Corpus Christi Day parades were more important for the church as a whole. They became increasingly elaborate instruments and expressions of the Catholic Reformation, inviting all and sundry to parade their Catholic identity by exhibiting samples of their crafts or some other identifying symbol of their everyday occupations. Celebration of Corpus Christi day had begun in the thirteenth century, but it assumed an entirely new scale and social significance in Seville and other Spanish cities during the sixteenth century. By the 1590s, the bishop of Seville's effort to make his city's festival the most magnificent in the world expanded the Corpus Christi celebration to embrace an entire week, involving all the citizens in festive dances, parades, and as spectators of others' performances.[38] In subsequent generations, elaborated forms of this springtime festival spread to Italy and then to the Hapsburg territories north of the Alps in the wake of Spanish arms and reforming piety. In German lands it soon became the principal and most conspicuous annual public affirmation of Catholic identity—a role Corpus Christi day parades retain to the present in the cities of Germany.

Protestant communities never developed a counterpart to Corpus Christi day parades. Insofar as piety over and above routine conformity to the requirements of public law survived among Lutherans and Calvinists, it became private and personal. Anabaptist congregations lived on, half-hidden from persecuting magistrates; and Hussites, whose persecution for heresy antedated the Reformation by a century, re-emerged in the 1720s when they discovered safe refuge on the estates of an especially pious Lutheran, Count Nikolaus von Zinzendorf. Much was secret and remains unknown, at least to me, until the Puritan-led revolution of seventeenth-century England once again allowed radical Protestant piety to find public expression.

On that occasion, millenary expectations, transmitted by scripture from the earliest days of the Christian church, flared up anew, and sects like those derisively dubbed Ranters and Diggers exhibited a great variety of muscular agitation that both expressed and invited visitations of the Holy Spirit. When actually attained, possession by the Holy Spirit was, by definition, an individual experience; but such experiences emerged from a background of congregational excitement aroused by singing, preaching, and erratic muscular manifestations of the Spirit that presumably took loosely defined rhythmic forms. But exactly what happened among such sects is hard to say, since historical investigation has concentrated on words and doctrines, not on details of congregational behavior.[39]

Baptists of the English-speaking world descend from these seventeenth-century enthusiasts; so do the Quakers, who acquired their nickname because of the muscular manifestations of private inspiration that once distinguished them from less incandescent believers. The name remains in common usage, even though silent meetings and restrained testimony from decorous members of the Meeting long ago supplanted the extreme and unpredictable expressions of red-hot emotion that once justified it.

In the absence of forcible repression, a natural succession obviously prevails whereby emotionally vibrant, innovative, and attractive sects either wear themselves out after a few excited years or else cool down, introduce limits upon individual expression of private inspiration, and begin to resemble older, more hierarchical branches of the Christian church. This started to happen among the Quakers during the lifetime of their founder, George Fox (d. 1691); and when the Act of Toleration halted official persecution in 1689, a quiet future dawned for most Quaker meetings that still endures.[40]

Nevertheless, sparks from the religious enthusiasm that flared so high in England between 1640 and 1660 lit a few fires elsewhere. The pietist movement among Lutherans in Germany, for instance, was partly inspired by English examples; and after Pietists attained a firm institutional base at the University of Halle, their effort to cultivate a "religion of the heart" opened a path for unruly, sporadic outbreaks of private inspiration once again. More important were a few dedicated Christian communities, like the Moravian Brethren established by Count von Zinzendorf on his estates in Saxony. They soon became energetic missionaries; and it was when meeting with a group of Moravian Brethren in London in 1738 that John Wesley's heart was "strangely warmed"—an experience that impelled him to develop what became Methodism in the English-speaking world.

It used to be thought that a far more surprising link existed between English millenarianism and a messianic upheaval among the Jews of eastern Europe provoked by the career of Sabbatai Sevi (1626–76). Sabbatai Sevi began life as a son of a Jewish merchant who had dealings with England's Levant company in Smyrna, but there is no evidence that English ideas about the Second Coming had anything to do with Sabbatai Sevi's belief that he was the long-awaited Messiah. His ideas fundamentally derived from Jewish mystical and kabbalistic traditions of long standing; and this tradition, in turn, made the claim plausible when a follower and admirer proclaimed him the Messiah at Jerusalem in 1665. Popular excitement soon led Ottoman authorities to intervene, offering him a choice between execution and conversion to Islam. When the supposed Messiah accepted conversion, a few followers imitated his example, thus founding a Moslem sect that persisted into the twentieth century.[41]

The surge of excitement provoked by Sabbatai Sevi's messianic claim spread far beyond Ottoman boundaries, raising a particularly intense response (and subsequent repudiation) in Jewish communities of Russia and Poland. When confusion settled down, a new, emotionally vibrant popular path to God, known as Hasidism, emerged to challenge the older, more intellectual, and narrowly scriptural style of Talmudic piety. It featured vigorously rhythmic prayer and community dancing that offended the conservative Jews of Poland and Lithuania profoundly.[42] Ba'al Shem Tov (d. ca. 1760) was the figure around whom this new, enthusiastic form of Judaism coalesced, and tales that his followers came to treasure emphasized the joy of dancing and its holy function of lifting the heart to God. His great-grandson once affirmed that the "way to set the heart on fire for God is by motion"; another defender of Hasidic piety even declared: "Prayer is copulation" and explicitly compared bodily motions in prayer with the sexual act.[43] Hasidic stories clustered around especially holy religious teachers, whose dancing gave uninhibited expression to their religious exaltation. For instance, it was said of one such teacher: "His feet were as light as those of a four year old. And not a single one of those who saw the holy dance failed to turn to God in that very instance, and with his whole soul, for he stirred the hearts of all who beheld him to both tears and ecstasy."[44]

Jewish millenarian excitement in Poland and the Ukraine may have communicated itself also to Russian Orthodox Old Believers. They had compelling reasons to expect the speedy end of the world after 1667, when a council of the Russian church endorsed innovations in Orthodox worship and simultaneously deposed the Patriarch Nikon, who had initiated them. The resulting schism in Russia was as significant for the subsequent history of that country as the Protestant Reformation was further west; but I have not found any discussion of dancing or other muscular expressions of collective excitement among the Old Believers, apart from their occasional resort to burning themselves alive in fortified churches when attacked by the tsar's armies.[45]

Sporadic outbreaks of intense religious excitement, each taking its own path and feeding on local tradition and circumstances, continued to occur among Christians from the eighteenth century onwards. Millenarian expectations were easily fanned into flame whenever an energetic preacher encountered an anxious and distressed congregation. On such occasions rhythmic muscular movements, ranging from vigorous hand clapping that set the beat for congregational hymn-singing to bodily convulsions, glossolalia, and trances, became standard. John Wesley (d. 1791) and other Methodist preachers institutionalized this style of religious revivalism in the English-speaking world. Enthusiastic meetings, initially outdoors, featured impassioned preaching and congregational hymn-singing, reinforced by hand clapping and rhythmic body movements. The desired and expected outcome was ecstatic visitations by the Holy Spirit for a few, and heartfelt repentance, together with healing emotional catharsis, for all.

Methodism attracted a large following from the new industrial working class of England and Wales, and swiftly became thoroughly respectable, though not, perhaps, as staid as the Quakers. But in the United States, where displaced persons abounded throughout the eighteenth and nineteenth centuries, an unending stream of new sects continued to emerge from recurrent waves of religious ethusiasm.[46] Two such sects, the Shakers and the Mormons—to use their colloquial names—are particularly interesting because of the different ways they institutionalized congregational dancing.

Dancing began among both groups as a frenetic, disorderly manifestation of the Spirit. As such, it could not be disdained nor suppressed outright. But from confused, anarchic beginnings, authorities of the two communities quickly devised ways of preserving or even of encouraging dancing, while restraining excessive and improper manifestations of the excitement it generated.

The United Society of Believers in Christ's Second Coming, to give the Shakers their official name, made dancing into a regular ritual. Founded in 1776, when Ann Lee of Manchester and eight of her disciples arrived in upstate New York, the Shakers organized themselves after her death in 1784 into tight-knit communites where they lived, worked, and worshiped together. For several decades they attracted a substantial number of recruits to their communal life despite (or perhaps because of) the strict celibacy imposed upon them. A mix of commercial shrewdness in dealings with the outside world and a rigorously disciplined community life, featuring hard work and meticulous craftsmanship, was relieved by ecstatic excitement aroused by dancing together at night. This blend of opposites proved viable through the first half of the nineteenth century. But new rules established stricter decorum in 1845, after some exceptionally fervent outbreaks, whereupon the constant recruitment needed to maintain numbers began to flag and the sect is now extinct. But for a while the emotional warmth sustained by dancing, together with a vivid belief in the imminent Second Coming of Christ, allowed Shaker communities to flourish and create the simple yet elegant furniture and other handicraft objects for which they are now famous.

The warm emotional residue of dancing was probably central to the sect's viability. Otherwise, celibacy and the rigorous routine of daily tasks would scarcely have been bearable; yet, with a twist that is perhaps only to be expected, sometimes Shaker dancers skirted sexual arousal by dancing naked "to kill their pride," and also engaged in self-flagellation. Most of the time, however, according to a lapsed member who published an account of the sect in 1792, they merely jumped up and down, "moving about as thick as they can crowd, with extraordinary transport, singing, sometimes one at a time, and sometimes more than one, making a perfect charm."[47]

The Church of Jesus Christ of Latter Day Saints, as Mormons call themselves, took a different path by segregating worship from dancing instead of mingling them as the Shakers had done. Beginning at Nauvoo, Illinois, where the Mormons sought to settle between 1839–1844, believers were organized into wards of between one hundred and fifty and two hundred families. Weekly ward meetings involved theatricals, choral singing, and dances, which, according to the Mormons' principal historian, "capped every celebration and were the most important amusement in all early Mormon wards."[48] A few years after their arrival in Utah, Brigham Young, the man who led the Mormons to that refuge in 1846, referred to the attractions of dancing in a sermon, saying: "Suppose I should appoint a meeting for tonight, about a dozen would come without any candles. If I were to say—level this stand for the band that we may have a dance, they would bring their stoves from their wives' bedsides, and would dance all night, and the house would be filled to overflowing."[49] Dramatic performances and dancing remained "especially strong" in ward meetings as recently as 1950, but, according to another Mormon historian, dances have since "declined somewhat in importance."[50] This is an ill augury for the future, if I am right in supposing that the conspicuous vigor of Mormonism in our time rests as much on the emotional residues aroused by Saturday night dances attended by old and young in most Mormon wards as on anything that takes place at Sunday services in church.

Mormon missionaries continue to make converts in many different parts of the world, but the most successful form of Christianity in Third World countries today is Pentecostalism. This emerged as a distinct entity in the United States from among other enthusiastic churches when in 1901 students of the Bethel Bible College in Topeka, Kansas, started to speak with tongues like the first Christians, and understood their experience to be baptism by the Holy Spirit, come to save them from damnation. The phenomenon spread quickly and found a second powerful center in a church in the industrial slums of Los Angeles, where, beginning in 1906, a Black Pentecostal preacher attracted believers from all walks of life, rich and poor, Black, Latino, and Anglo. From this focus, Pentecostal inspiration spread into Mexico and other Latin American countries and subsequently took root also in Russia, England, Scandinavia, and South Africa. Glossolalia and the trance that sustains it remain central to the movement. Ritual healing of physical and mental ailments by expelling evil spirits is another conspicuous benefit that Pentecostal churches offer to their followers. Singing and congregational dancing supplement preaching and help to generate the ecstasy of trance.

Pentecostalists continue to give wide scope to individual inspiration, despite the difficulty of authenticating that it comes from God. Maintaining the emotional intensity at which outbreaks of glossolalia occur is difficult too; but as long as people suffer disappointment and hardship in their daily lives, the emotional release, healing of illnesses, and assurance of salvation through personal contact with God that Pentecostal churches provide allows them to flourish in much the same way that the earliest Christian churches presumably did in Roman times.[51]

Unlike most Christian fundamentalists, Pentecostalists invite the Spirit more than they invoke Scripture, with all the anarchic, innovative possibilities that this implies. That, I suspect, is why Pentecostal churches continue to meet with marked success in the Third World, though it seems quite improbable that their incandescence can be sustained indefinitely. Pressures to rein in some of the anarchic expressions of religious excitement have long been felt. In principle, conflict between Scripture and inspiration by the Holy Spirit is impossible, since God does not contradict Himself. In practice, however, the possibility of inspiration by an evil spirit requires someone to decide what is true and what is false. As a result, efforts to extirpate error and cooperate in spreading the Gospel have already

## The Sorcerer

This drawing of a painting on the walls of Trois Frères cave in southern France is the oldest record of what appears to be human dancing. The original was painted by Magdalenian hunters more than 11,000 years ago. The figure, which shows human legs supporting an animal body and a head with antlers and owl-like eyes, is reminiscent of how contemporary shamans of northern Asia sometimes dance, wearing animal masks, until they go into trance and, by their own account, enter the spirit world. Perhaps Magdalenian experts in the supernatural did the same. If so, this painting is also the oldest surviving evidence of how dance-trance, as interpreted afterwards in words, introduced religious meanings and sanctions into human experience. (Centre d'Etudes et Documentation Prehistoriques, Montignac)

## A Harvest Festival of Song—and Dance?

This fragment of a vase made in Minoan Crete about 1500 B.C. (known as the Harvester Vase) shows singers, mouths agape, with musical instruments and harvesting tools in their hands. Unfortunately, we cannot tell whether their feet were dancing—as seems probable—because only the top part of the original survives. It is nonetheless the oldest surviving artistic representation of a village festival. Such celebrations were universal among villagers in historic times, and the custom of community-wide dancing on festive occasions is probably as old as humankind itself. Extravagant expenditure of muscular energy in dance and song is the most fundamental of all human devices for consolidating community feeling, simply because it arouses a warm sense of togetherness, diminishing personal conflicts and facilitating cooperation. (Archaeological Museum, Heraklion/Archaeological Receipts Fund, Athens)

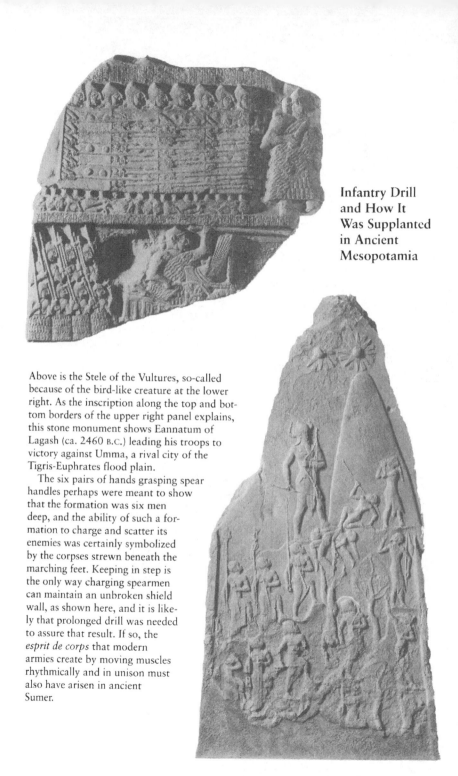

## Infantry Drill and How It Was Supplanted in Ancient Mesopotamia

Above is the Stele of the Vultures, so-called because of the bird-like creature at the lower right. As the inscription along the top and bottom borders of the upper right panel explains, this stone monument shows Eannatum of Lagash (ca. 2460 B.C.) leading his troops to victory against Umma, a rival city of the Tigris-Euphrates flood plain.

The six pairs of hands grasping spear handles perhaps were meant to show that the formation was six men deep, and the ability of such a formation to charge and scatter its enemies was certainly symbolized by the corpses strewn beneath the marching feet. Keeping in step is the only way charging spearmen can maintain an unbroken shield wall, as shown here, and it is likely that prolonged drill was needed to assure that result. If so, the *esprit de corps* that modern armies create by moving muscles rhythmically and in unison must also have arisen in ancient Sumer.

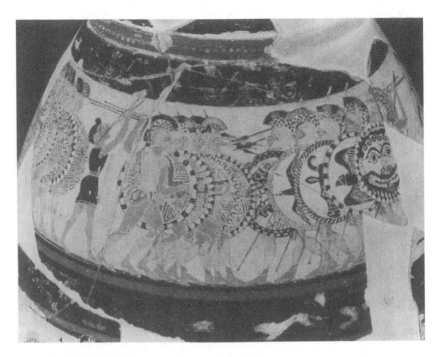

## Greek Phalanx Warfare

This vase, found near Rome in an Etruscan tomb, was made in Corinth just before 600 B.C. It offers one of the earliest and clearest depictions of phalanx warfare as practiced in ancient Greece. Rival ranks of shield-carrying warriors, wearing helmets and greaves for additional protection, approach each other, spears at the ready, while a flutist in the rear signals the attack. The way the feet and lower legs are depicted looks as though the hoplites on both sides were keeping in step, moving together to the sound of the flute. The advantage of keeping in step to assure an unbroken shield wall was obvious. The Spartans profited from doing so in the sixth and fifth centuries B.C., and later on, when the Macedonians and Romans professionalized warfare, marching in step became the norm. Prolonged practice drills created and sustained intense fellow-feeling among soldiers, insulating them from surrounding society in a fashion antithetical to the political involvement of the citizen-soldiers of an earlier age. (Scala/Art Resource, N.Y.)

(Infantry Drill, *continued*)
But massed infantry formations did not dominate Mesopotamian battlefields for very long, as the second stele shows. It was erected to celebrate how Naram Sin (ca. 2250 B.C.) defeated barbarians in some distant mountainous country. The king carries a bow whose reverse curve resembles the shape of powerful compound bows of later ages; and it is probable that Naram Sin's Akkadian ancestors, Semitic-speaking newcomers from the desert fringe of Mesopotamia, used such bows to attack and defeat massed Sumerian spearmen from a safe distance. Thereafter drill became useless; keeping together in time disappeared and so did the psychological cohesion it aroused. Instead, nimble, open-order formations, like what is shown here, supplanted Eannatum's style of fighting. (Louvre © Photo R.M.N.)

## A Flemish Wedding Dance

Pieter Brueghel the Elder painted this famous scene of peasant life in 1566. By that time, Flemish artists and patrons were so thoroughly urbanized that they began to feel interest in, and nostalgia for, a simpler world preserved among rural folk. Always before, scenes from peasant life had been judged inappropriate for fine art.

If we compare this painting with the Harvester Vase and take note of what modern anthropologists report about village-wide dancing in isolated communities, signs of the incipient disruption of community solidarity become obvious: men and women are dancing in couples, and not everyone is dancing. By the sixteenth century, European villages were beginning to merge into an urban-based society where community-wide dancing and the cohesion it generated could no longer be taken for granted, and where upper-class styles of courtly dance and sexual pairing-off had begun to infiltrate peasant behavior on festival occasions. (Photo © The Detroit Institute of Arts, 1995. City of Detroit Purchase)

## Revived Infantry Drill, East and West

At the same time that Brueghel's painting indicated incipient disruption of village communities in western Europe, new-fangled styles of infantry drill introduced a remarkable simulacrum of village community solidarity among companies of infantrymen. Although no one intended such an effect, well-drilled soldiers created a strong sense of solidarity with their fellows simply by moving in unison. These two diagrams record the almost simultaneous revival of infantry drill in the Far East and Far West of Eurasia.

The top diagram is from a recent edition (1937) of a book by the Chinese military reformer, Ch'i Chi-kuang (1528–1587). It shows how to form a lager of wagons for protection against attacking nomads. Using such tactics, Chinese armies could move safely across open grasslands as never before, conquering the eastern half of the Eurasian steppe by 1757 and creating the imperial state that still exists. (Harvard Yenching Library)

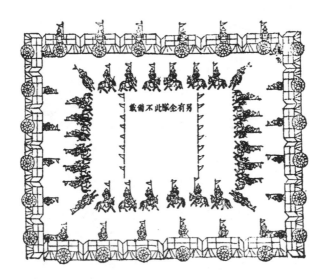

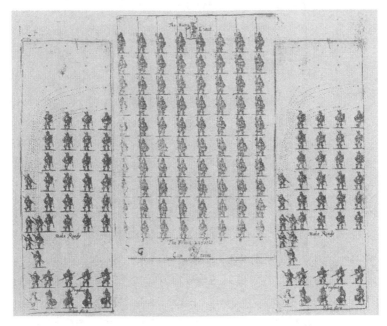

Simultaneously, Russian soldiers also subdued steppe peoples, approaching them from the other flank, by using techniques of drill and deployment pioneered by Maurice of Orange, Captain-General of Holland between 1585 and 1625. The bottom diagram shows how Maurice's drill prepared a company of 160 men—half carrying pikes, half armed with cumbersome hand guns—to advance against the enemy. The "sleeves" of arquebusiers on either flank of the pikemen send two ranks forward to aim and fire. Then they fall back while two more ranks advance to take their place. All the while, ranks in the rear are kept busy performing the complicated sequence of prescribed motions needed to prepare their guns for firing. (University of Illinois Library)

## Muscular Mass Politics, Nazi Style

Adolf Hitler (1889–1945) consciously experimented with muscular techniques for provoking a passionate collective response among his followers, and eventually perfected the art to such a degree that the German nation blindly followed him into war in 1939 and remained obedient until almost the very end.

Here the Hitler Youth Color Guard at the Nuremberg Party Rally marches in front of a crowd of other uniformed members of that organization. The long vista of arms raised in the Hitler salute, and the anxious, alert postures of those close enough to the camera to be clearly discernible, suggest the intensity of such occasions. Individuals eagerly merged into a like-feeling mass, and, excited by moving together, became intoxicated by a sense of their irresistible strength. It is no exaggeration to say that this sort of muscular movement *en masse* undergirded the whole of Hitler's political success. (UPI/Bettmann Newsphotos)

# A Contemporary Muscular Expression of Religious Enthusiasm

These worshippers at an outdoor gathering in Rio de Janeiro are Pentecostalists. They value "speaking in tongues" that accompanies trance as a sign that the Holy Spirit has come to visit the person so affected; and, as this photograph shows, they invite such visitations by singing and praying together and engaging in rhythmic bodily movements.

As the figure of the Sorcerer in Trois Frères cave suggests, trance-dance as a mode of communication with supernatural spirits is very old indeed. It remains alive and vigorous today among religious sects of every persuasion and has especial resonance among the poor of Third World cities. Religious worship is, in fact, one of the principal ways in which the emotional arousal of keeping together in time has found constructive expression in the human past. Obviously, it continues to do so. (Nair/Benedicto/N Imagens S/C. Ltda.)

## Industrial Calisthenics in Japan

This photo, taken in the 1980s at Asahikawa on Japan's northern island of Hokkaido, shows how employees of a Coca Cola bottling plant prepare for their day's work by engaging in calisthenic exercises. Calisthenics were imported into Japan (and China) from Europe, where they had been developed in the nineteenth century.

Such public muscular exercises built directly on long-standing Buddhist reliance on rhythmic movement for spiritual purification. But European-style calisthenics soon acquired other meanings. After 1867, Japanese schools used calisthenics to turn their pupils into patriotic subjects of the restored Emperor; and after World War II, factories sought to instill loyalty among their employees by beginning the day with exercises like those shown here. In both instances, calisthenics presumably confirmed common feeling and improved cooperation among all who took part. (Diego Goldberg/Sygma) resulted in the establishment of at least four rival Pentecostal associations based in the United States. Nonetheless, spontaneity still prevails in innumerable churches and conventicles.[52]

Pentecostalism in Latin America probably draws on Amerindian shamanist styles of inspiration as well as on the Christian past. Far more obvious forms of religious syncretism have met with much success in Brazil and Africa, and some new groups rely very much on dancing to define what membership means. Let me say a few words about only two of them: what is known as Umbanda in Brazil, and the Nazaretha church founded in South Africa by "Zulu Christ" Johannes Galilee Shemba (1870–1935).

Like Pentecostalism, Umbanda centers on spiritual possession, though the spirits that visit those who attend Umbanda meetings are not divine but quite ordinary humans—male and female, slave and free, saints, naughty children, and various other humble persons. Umbanda seems to have started in Rio de Janeiro and São Paulo in the 1920s. A national federation was organized in 1941, and by 1961 had sufficient following to fill a vast outdoor stadium in Rio for an annual meeting and even to elect two members to Parliament. Yet what happens at Umbanda meetings depends on what the local cult leader and followers decide, and variation from group to group and time to time is taken for granted.

Spiritualism, imported from France in the mid-nineteenth century, was one antecedent to Umbanda; but its ceremonials derive largely from African and Amerindian religious rituals, though Roman Catholic motifs are not necessarily absent. The cult leaders are self-appointed and make a modest living by collecting dues from those who come to their meetings. In return, the cult delivers messages from the spirits through mediums who enter into trance at cult meetings with the help of drumming, song, dance, and prayer. Once possessed, the mediums speak and act in ways appropriate to the spirit in question—wicked or saintly, old or young as the case may be—and can transmit questions from onlookers and receive answers from the spirit world. Ordinary onlookers sing and dance too, and may sometimes be possessed; but most are content to observe the often lively, quasi-dramatic perform- ances of the mediums, and relieve their anxieties by finding out what the spirits will tell them to do about personal problems of any and every kind.[53]

Umbanda cult centers obviously help lost souls to make their way in the cold impersonality of a big city. Dance and drums play a very prominent part in Umbanda meetings, and the warm emotional response to keeping time together surely sup- plements all the meanings expressed in words. Such mingling of bodily and verbal communication is indeed characteristic of all public religious observances. What distinguishes Umbanda and other religions influenced from Africa is the prominence of dance and drums. This is also true of the Nazaretha church, founded in 1911 by J. G. Shemba, whose religion, according to a sympathetic Lutheran observer, was "not so much thought out as danced out."[54]

Shemba was baptized into the African Native Baptist Church in 1906 but struck out on his own in 1911, founding a new church and developing new, distinctive rituals. He or- ganized the principal festival of the year on top of a mountain, where it lasted for two weeks. Prayer, healing, ceremonial offerings, and other sacred rituals took place each day, cli- maxing with a dance, led by the prophet himself, that lasted, with some intervals of rest, for two climactic days. "The whole ensemble—the offering, the sacrifices, the hymns, the rhythm of the drums, the dancing and above all the presence of the healing prophet himself on that high and holy moun- tain—creates an atmosphere which surpasses anything else in the Nazarite ritual. The service on the mountain brings them very near to heaven, they feel."[55]

After Shemba's death in 1935, his son succeeded him and encouraged the view that his father had been no ordinary man, saying to an inquirer: "Who Shemba was I do not know. . . . He was born of the Spirit and was the Spirit. He was the Sent, sent to the Bantus and to all nations." A female follower was more explicit when she said: "Jesus we have only seen in photos. But I know Shemba and I believe in him. He is the one who created heaven and earth; he is God for us Black people."[56]

Christian motifs are obvious; equally obvious is the fact that Shemba's ritual dancing on the mountain top sacralized what had been military-political forms of leadership in the Zulu past. At the top of the mountain, Shemba divided his followers by age and status into separate dance groups. Old men, married women, girls and boys: each danced in separate formation and wore distinctive costumes as well. Shaka Zulu (1787–1828) had organized his warriors along similar lines, dividing them into age classes, each distinguished by its own pattern of shield decoration. He trained them for battle by leading them in dance, just as Shemba was later to lead his followers to Heaven. Thus Christian ideas united with local tradition gave the sect a unique character and considerable influence among the Zulu people.[57] And once again it seems safe to assume that the emotional effect of keeping together in time played a large part in sustaining the sect's cohesion and its power to alter members' lives.

After focusing attention on these contemporary sects that make much of dancing, it is perhaps well to correct the balance by remarking again that, for the Christian church as a whole, dance has not had much importance. Scripture and doctrine was what mattered for most Christians, and muscular expression of religious emotion was usually confined to a few pre-scribed ritual gestures. Yet over and over again, in times of trouble and among distressed populations, preaching and song combined with rhythmic muscular movements to provoke fresh inspiration. So despite the dominant distrust of danc-ing—holy and otherwise—inspiration from below, provoked by preaching, song, and dance, constituted a very significant growth point for Christianity, recurrently challenging and renewing established hierarchical churches of every creed.

For moslems, the primacy of Scripture was even greater than for Jews and Christians, though of course the Moslem sacred Scripture was the new revelation of the Koran, sent by God specifically to to correct the errors that had crept into Jewish and Christian sacred books. Moreover, to combat a number of would-be imitators of Mohammed, the early Moslem community emphatically declared that the Prophet's death had closed the Gate of Prophecy. Nonetheless, there is a muscular side to Moslem worship that may have played an important part in keeping the early community together: to wit, the prescribed ritual of prayer which required assembled believers to bow before God, repeatedly acknowledging His greatness by touching foreheads to the ground while uttering the words "God is Great." Performed together five times a day, in a rhythm defined by the summons and example of the prayer leader (initially, Mohammed himself), and lasting for several minutes each time, this sort of prayer obviously required Moslems to move rhythmically and in unison. It is possible (though not proved) that public demonstration of membership in the Community of the Faithful in this fashion may have had the incidental effect of arousing emotional warmth and solidarity similar to that associated with drill and dancing.

This is an attractive hypothesis, because what made the Moslems so surprisingly successful in the first decades of their history was the extraordinary way the new faith proved capable of transcending ancient tribal rivalries. The revelation of God's will to Mohammed was the initial stimulus, and subsequent victories in battle obviously helped to unite the Arab tribes under the banner of Islam. Yet even though the rise of Islam offers perhaps the most impressive example in world history of the power of words to alter human behavior in sudden, surprising ways, it is also possible that Islam's initial success also reflected a new emotional solidarity within the Community of the Faithful arising from the muscular unison of public prayer.

No one has considered this possibility, and intrinsically it seems impossible to test. Contemporary Moslems, even if they were willing to analyze their own emotional responses to public prayer, cannot reproduce the conditions of the early Community, when Mohammed's revelation was new and converts had to repudiate former identities and loyalties when they accepted Islam. In such a situation, solidarity provoked by keeping together in time can make previously disparate persons into a spirited group, as Saul discovered in his time and as innumerable drill sergeants have proved in modern armies. Something analogous may have occurred among the Moslems who gathered at Medina and launched Islam on its world career.

Assuredly, early Islamic victories puzzle all who do not believe that it was God's will. The most obvious natural explanation of the Byzantine and Persian defeats is that the fighting manpower of all Arabia was combined under one command, as never before or since. Undoubtedly, Sacred Scripture and verbal agreements provided a basis for cooperation, but perhaps only a part.[58] And even after the initial unity broke down, permitting political rivals to divide the Community, the daily ritual of prayer (together with the duty of going on pilgrimage to Mecca and Medina at least once in a lifetime for all who can afford it) continued to unite Moslems both in their local congregations and throughout the realm of Islam. Everywhere, daily prayer continues to be the most conspicuous outward mark distinguishing Moslems from unbelievers. Directed towards Mecca, the ritual of prayer symbolically unites Moslems in every continent every day. Hence even when doctrinal controversy divided Islam into the "two and seventy jarring sects" that Omar Khayyam (d. 1131)[59] derided in his quatrains, muscular expression of the unity of Islam remained undiminished, and will surely continue to do so into the future.

The rise of dervish orders offers a second example of how muscular expressions of religious emotion supplemented the scriptural rigor of Islam. The distinguishing feature of dervish forms of piety was that initiates sought direct communion with God; but the exact paths they took varied enormously. In conformity with Indian yoga traditions for pursuing holiness, intense bonding between master and disciple was common. Private bodily discipline, like fasting and breath control, or, alternatively, using drugs like hashish, sometimes helped to induce the mystic state. But chanting holy formulas for hours on end, often accompanied by flute and drum, was by far the most common way to seek mystic union with God.[60]

Only in one order, the Mevlevi, was more strenuous dancing of major importance. This order was founded at Konya, the Seljuk Turkish capital, by the poet and mystic Jalaluddin Rumi (1207–1273). Rumi's poems elaborate endlessly on how the soul's ascent to God is like a lover seeking his beloved. The emotional resonance of such piety attracted a considerable following in his lifetime, and the Mevlevi order they formed after his death still survives. Westerners called its members whirling or dancing dervishes because of their custom of dancing in public, whirling round and round and chanting all the while, until, after achieving the mystic state, they collapse at the feet of their master who, standing upright in the center and constituting the pole of the dance, shares in the rapture while he supervises the rite.[61]

Beginning about the year 1000, the emotion generated by the dervishes' personal encounter with God challenged older forms of Islamic learning and piety. Dervishes often hovered on the verge of heresy, and some were executed for disregarding points of sacred law as defined by official interpretations of the Koran. Yet most accepted the established prescriptions of the faith. Living familiarly with God and enjoying a close connection with the general public, whose gifts sustained them, they infused a new intensity of religious conviction into Moslem society at large, and sustained a remarkable surge of missionary expansion across every frontier of the Islamic world. Islamic missionary successes still persist in parts of Asia and Africa and, for that matter, in the urban jungles of the United States of America, where some groups of Black Moslems have evolved from an idiosyncratic, autonomous sect (founded in 1930) into a self-consciously orthodox Moslem community.[62]

The dervishes also created a powerful new element in Moslem society that disdained the path of reason as mere playing with words, valuing instead their own emotionally charged, direct encounter with God. This inhibited intelligent reaction to important novelties like the discovery of America, and seriously handicapped the Islamic world in trying to cope with western encroachment in subsequent centuries. But in the short run the effect was exactly opposite. Dervish nearness to God made them effective missionaries, and dervish enthusiasm inspired Moslem armies to undertake new conquests across almost every frontier. As a result, between 1000 and 1700 the realm of Islam expanded enormously—sweeping across India and parts of southeast Asia, across Asia Minor and the Balkans, as well as penetrating east and west Africa, northwest China, and most of the Eurasian steppe.[63]

I conclude that it is difficult to exaggerate the impact of dervish forms of piety on Islamic society in the centuries after 900. Everything turned on the emotional conviction aroused by mystic union with God; and that union was achieved through prolonged chanting, with a background of instrumental music and varying levels of rhythmic muscular engagement. Twice, therefore, muscular unison among Moslems appears to have altered the course of world history: once among the Community of the Faithful in its earliest days, binding uprooted individuals into a new social entity, and again among innumerable dervish subcommunities. These events were almost as world-shaking as ecstatic prophecy among the ancient Hebrews had been in its time. That is because the civilizational boundaries that divide humankind today were shaped very largely by emotional ties and convictions aroused among these small groups of men, all seeking direct contact with God, each in its own way.

Thus it appears that despite the conscious, deliberate effort of all pious Moslems to discover and obey God's will as recorded in Sacred Scripture, words were only part of what united them. Keeping together in time, along with music, song, and chant, also played its part, arousing primitive, inchoate, and powerful sentiments of solidarity that allowed them to act more energetically and effectively than words and doctrine by themselves could have done.

It is very probable that the mystic path followed by Moslem dervishes was influenced by the example of Indian holy men, whose yoga, as mentioned already, also helped to shape the beginnings of Christian monasticism. The Upanishads show that private and personal techniques for inducing trance developed luxuriantly in India as early as 800 B.C., along with the custom of forming discipleships in forest retreats around particularly adept holy men. Techniques for inducing trance were readily exportable, and if my remarks about Christian and Moslem mysticism are well founded, the example set by Indian holy men extended far and wide.

Indian transcendental piety took a somewhat more structured form when disciples of Gautama Buddha (d. ca. 483 B.C.) agreed to rules for their pursuit of holiness, gathering for part of the year in what we call monasteries where they could support each other in striving for full and final enlightenment. In subsequent centuries, monastic Buddhism spread into central and southeast Asia, China, and Japan, but almost disappeared from India itself owing to the upsurge of what we call Hinduism.

This religious history generated a vast number of texts whose doctrinal complexities have only been partially deciphered by historians of religion. Little is known about the merely muscular behavior associated with the diverse doctrines of Indian religions. In general, it is safe to say that they were far more hospitable to dancing than Judaism, Christianity, and Islam—the three religions of the Book. After all, according to later legend, the great God Shiva danced to create the world. On a more mundane, historical level, it seems probable that the eclipse of Buddhism in India and the emergence of Hinduism from a confused multiplicity of local cults in the early centuries of the Christian era depended very largely on enthusiasm generated at public assemblies, where everyone present united in dance, song, and processionals honoring one or another divinity. This supplemented and popularized the emotional effect of professional dancing before cult statues, which remained a prominent part of temple rituals and probably descended from very ancient times—perhaps from the time of the Indus civilization itself.

The ritual elaboration of Hinduism was, of course, accompanied by the composition of texts that set out to define the meaning of priestly and popular acts of worship. But it seems likely that rituals inviting enthusiastic muscular expression of religious feeling among the populace at large led the way, and literary interpretation of how different kinds of worship in different communities could be fittted together only came afterwards. "In the beginning was the act" is perhaps a better description of Indian religious history than "In the beginning was the word."[64]

In more recent centuries the career of Chaitanya (d. 1534) illustrates how important feelings of solidarity generated by public worship, music, and dance were for Hinduism. Chaitanya was an itinerant holy man whose public career centered in Bengal, where his extraordinary muscular contortions and esctatic praise for Krishna attracted crowds that soon recognized him as the living embodiment of the God he worshipped. God in the flesh was no common thing, even in India; and the excitement he communicated to his followers united them so warmly that all distinctions of caste were wiped away.

This, in turn, had the effect of checking conversion to Islam in the frontier zone of eastern Bengal. Before Chaitanya's time, large numbers of forest peoples in process of being folded into Indian society had been attracted to Islam, because Hindus consigned them to the lowest castes. But once welcomed as equals into an enthusiastic Hindu community, they preferred the mystic, muscular encounter with a living God that Chaitanya and his followers offered them. Thus, just as the spread of hesychasm among Greek Orthodox clergy had once checked wholesale conversion to Islam in the Balkans, Chaitanya's revivalism, together with subsequent literary definitions of popular Hindu piety by the poets Sur Das (d. 1563) and Tulsi Das (d. 1627), rendered Hinduism nearly proof against Moslem and Christian missionaries even though (or perhaps because) they were backed first by India's Moslem and then by its British rulers.[65]

In this instance we know for sure that public ritual and muscularly induced excitement led the way, and written texts followed after. For earlier centuries one can only suspect that the hymns and other sacred writings celebrating and commenting on mystical identification with Shiva, Krishna, or some other divine avatar were composed only after public ritual practices had made personal union with the divine a popular and practicable ideal.

I conclude that publicly shared dance and song supplemented more specialized private forms of yoga to give the Indian religions their distinctive character. Muscularly expressed and generated emotions mattered far more than they did for religions of the Book; and the historical ebbs and flows of such emotion did much to establish existing geographical boundaries among the world's higher religions.[66]

As for Buddhists in the Far East and southeast Asia, I have not discovered accounts either of monastic routines or of popular piety that cast light on muscular or musical expressions of enthusiasm among them. After 843 A.D., when the Chinese court dissolved all the monasteries under its jurisdiction, Buddhism was relegated to the margins of Chinese society, often taking the form of semi-secret associations, some of which stood in conscious opposition to the state. Among such groups disciples were linked to masters both by verbal teaching and by muscular forms of apprenticeship and initiation; but what really went on is unknowable. Peasant rebellions often took on a Buddhist coloration; and one such even eventuated in the establishment of the Ming dynasty (1368–1644).[67] Fragmentary and obscure information about the background of the Boxer Uprising of 1899 offers the best available insight into the way underground, quasi-Buddhist associations flared up in times of trouble; but of course the exact details of the Boxer movement were unique, even if the pattern of its propagation through the countryside and the mingling of naive, superstitious ideas with muscular exercises, climaxing in spiritual possession, were probably shared by other, earlier groups.[68]

The Confucian establishment that ruled China through most of its history put enormous store on rites. These were decorous, quasi-religious observances with a very considerable muscular component; but like the sedate gestures prescribed by the liturgy of established Christian churches, Confucian rituals, though they sometimes did involve dancing, were not such as to arouse strong emotions. They did affirm and in some part also created hierarchical relations among the persons participating in such ceremonies, and linked the living with their departed ancestors. Appropriate rites also established proper relations with other spirits, all the way up to the topmost T'ien or Heaven. Some were public, some *were* confined to the imperial palace, and some took place in private family gatherings.

Words and gestures made a seamless whole, reinforcing all the customary relationships of Chinese society. But like the established forms of Christian and Moslem worship, Confucian rites tended to ossify. Innovation from below in China came from Taoist, Buddhist, and also perhaps from shamanist practices. Changes derived from these sources did filter into Confucian rites across the centuries; but the social distance between dignified Confucians and dissenting religious groups in China was clearly greater than the differences between defenders of the established order and would-be reformers both in Christendom and in the realm of Islam, if only because in China there was no shared scripture to which all adhered.[69]

In Japan muscular expression of religious enthusiasm was especially associated with the Nichiren form of Buddhism, founded in the thirteenth century. It took root among rebellious peasants and suffered sporadic persecution by public authorities in subsequent centuries before taking on new life in the 1920s, when the sect's leaders established a society for laymen called Soka Gakkai. Suppressed once again during World War II, Soka Gakkai was refounded in 1945 and grew very rapidly, claiming eight million members in Japan by 1987 with an additional 1.3 million in other countries.[70] Members of Soka Gakkai demonstrate their religious identity daily by engaging in congregational exercises in public places, and the society also stages enormous annual festivals that remind unfriendly observers of Hitler's Nuremberg rallies. On these occasions, crowds of up to 80,000 assemble in an open air stadium where they engage in mass calisthenics, applaud dancers and marching bands, and, on the appropriate signal, unite in lifting colored placards high above their heads, thus giving shape to appropriate slogans when viewed from the other side of the stadium. The meeting comes to its climax when the sect's leader, Ikeda Daisaku, appears and exhorts them to labor even harder towards "The Third Civilization" that Soka Gakkai aspires to bring to all the world.

As always, it is words that carry the Soka Gakkai message, but leaders of the sect in the postwar years deliberately cultivated the emotional effect of mass movement in unison, and did so in spectacular ways. A factor in the situation is that Buddhism has no God; hence recitation of phrases from the Lotus Sutra to the accompaniment of dramatic muscular gestures was all that Ikeda and his predecessors had to build upon. Appealing as they do to newly urbanized masses in the cities of Japan, the muscular modernity of Soka Gakkai's festivals smacks more of American football crowds than of Hitler's Nazis. But in the postwar decades this odd sort of religious syncretism went from strength to strength, and the muscular manifestations of group identity, which play such a prominent part in its public rituals, contributed mightily to the movement's extraordinary success.[71]


THESE OBSERVATIONS about the muscular component of religious enthusiasm are both superficial and incomplete. Most historians of religion have paid little attention to this side of their subject; and written sources remain sketchy before modern times, when travelers' tales and anthropological accounts make information about religious dance, song, and trance more fully accessible. But poor and distressed people for whom ecstatic behavior is especially attractive—since it allows them to escape from the difficulties and disapointments of daily life, at least for a while—do not usually write about their experiences or describe the muscular behavior that brings on the mystic state. Ignorance of much that took place is therefore likely to remain, even if scholars were to search available records more energetically than hitherto. Yet it is in such contexts that keeping together in time played its principal role in urban, civilized history—partly by reconciling the poor and

disinherited to their lot, partly by challenging constituted religious and political authority, and partly by reforming and renewing established forms of worship.

Just as continental drift causes perpetual upwelling of
magma along the mid-Atlantic trench, so, beginning in the
second millennium B.C., the inequities of civilized society provoked recurrent upwellings of religious excitement at the bottom of society. Continental drift demonstrates its awesome
power by causing earthquakes from time to time. With similar
unpredictability, religious enthusiasts may also occasionally
provoke violent outbursts of rebellion and revolution. Under
such circumstances, religion passes over into politics; and in the
next chapter I will follow suit, turning attention to some of the
political and military manifestations of the human susceptibil-
ity for acting on emotions aroused by keeping together in time.

# Politics and War

POPULAR EMOTION and the rhythmic muscular expressions of group excitement that played so considerable a part in religion seldom affected politics before modern times. Instead, court ceremonies supported the status quo by using a variety of muscular actions that were calculated to express the dignity and power of rulers, and to reinforce appropriate subordination on the part of everyone else. Dancing was sometimes part of court ceremony; military display was almost always present; but the heights of ecstasy that play so important a role in religion were too unpredictable to be safely called upon. Military parades, stately processionals, formal audiences, and occasional appearances before a thronging crowd kept carefully at a distance: these were the characteristic expressions of political ritual in the deeper past. Rhythmic movement sometimes figured in courtly ceremonials but seldom mattered much. Enthusiasm and spontaneity were inappropriate. Playing an assigned role with practiced precision was what mattered.

Such behavior undoubtedly stabilized the existing political order, just as religious ceremonies did. Courtiers, officials, and the general public felt and thought differently because of their participation in these rituals.[1] That, undoubtedly, is why they were so meticulously elaborated throughout the civilized world. But until the time of the French Revolution, or thereabouts, politics had no equivalent to the religious enthusiasm that continually challenged and renewed religious establishments from below. Instead of finding overtly political expression, popular discontent tended to fuel sectarian forms of religion. Overt challenge to constituted authority was far too dangerous for ordinary people to contemplate. Muscular affirmation of group identity for political purposes was correspondingly inhibited, even though religious groups sometimes did provoke revolutions, as we saw in the preceding chapter.

The role of keeping time together in war was different. Hand-to-hand combat inevitably involved strenuous muscular exertion; and preparation for fighting, followed by victory celebration afterwards, often, perhaps always, involved special war dances. Such dances heightened excitement and had the practical advantage of consolidating fellow-feeling among the fighters. Combat efficiency could be increased in other ways as well. Mimicry of battle might teach the proper use of weapons and strengthen endurance in the field. Discipline and morale could be enhanced by honoring heroes with solo performances to show off some of their past feats. And by working themselves up to a state of extreme excitement, warriors could sometimes mount reckless attacks and tip the balance between victory and defeat. Moros in the Philippines amazed American soldiers by such behavior as recently as 1911;[2] Viking berserkers had done the same in Europe a millennium before.

War dances were almost universal among simple and barbarian societies. For example, according to Tacitus, the Germans of his day had only one kind of public amusement on festival occasions. "Naked youths, who practice the sport, bound in the dance amid swords and lances that threaten their lives. Experience gives them skill, and skill again gives them grace; profit and pay are out of the question; however reckless their pastime, its reward is the pleasure of the spectators."[3] Scottish Highlanders persisted in similar exercises as recently as 1745, with the difference that they wore kilts and did without lances.

On the other side of the world, in 1859 Maoris prepared for war as follows: "With the regularity of a regiment at drill, each man elevated the right leg and the right side of his body, then the left leg and the left side, and then jumped two feet from the ground, brandishing his weapons and yelling a loud chorus."[4] Zulus, Swazis, and other African peoples still engage in war dances on festival occasions, and of late Zulu shield- and spear-bearing dancers have begun to appear on the world's TV screens when taking part in South African political demonstrations.[5]

A particularly interesting case is that of the Aztecs. They built their state and society on a partnership between priestly colleges and corporations of privileged warriors, whose rank and collective identity found expression in formalized dances. Young men who aspired to rank among the warriors began by attending special schools in Tenochtitlán. "The youth ate in his own home but was required to sleep in the school and work and associate with other . . . youths during the day. When the sun had set they started fires and danced until after midnight."[6] After a few years of this sort of preparation, military apprentices accompanied an experienced warrior into the field, and, as campaign succeeded campaign, began to climb the ranks by capturing enemies in battle. Careers were open to talent. Those who succeeded in capturing four enemies alive attained the highest military rank; but along the way, each successful foray into the field that resulted in bringing back another human sacrifice for the sun god resulted in promotion, signified by a dance at which the Aztec monarch awarded distinctive insignia to each successful warrior and promoted him to the next higher rank.[7]

Throughout the military career, dancing remained the way warriors asserted their corporate identity and prepared for battle. On the night before fighting broke out between Spaniards and Aztecs in Tenochtitlán, the Spaniards were alarmed by the noise of one such dance. A Spanish survivor, Antonio Herrara, described it as follows: "That night more than a thousand knights got together in the temple, with great loud sounds of drums, shrill trumpets, cornets and notched bones. . . . They danced nude . . . in a circle, holding their hands, in rows and keeping time to the tune of the musicians and singers."[8]

Spartans and Zulus developed similarly rigorous styles of military training, for they, too, required youths to live apart from others according to age classes and participate in physical exercises that combined dance with military drill.[9] These are the only examples I know of that come close to the Aztec way of ordering their society around military associations of warriors whose rank depended on demonstrated performance in battle. The uniqueness of the Aztec system rested on the fact that their military-political system was religious at the same time, for the professed purpose of warfare was to feed the sun god with enough human hearts to keep him strong against the forces of darkness. "War must always continue," according to an Aztec hymn, "so that each time and whenever we wish and our god wishes to eat and feast, we may go there as one who goes to market to buy something to eat . . . organized to obtain victories to offer our god Huitzilopochtli."[10]

Thus war and religion were one and the same. War dances were religious dances, performed to assure the gods' favor "by serving them and calling upon them with one's whole body."[11] Military campaigns had religious purposes. Government itself existed to serve the gods; and the rapid expansion of the radius of Aztec military operations after 1433 rested on a new religious idea as much as on their extraordinary way of training and rewarding specialized associations of warriors.[12] Dance was the main expression of the warriors' collective existence; but what looked like military practice to European outsiders was a form of worship for the dancers themselves.

The peculiar Aztec merger of religion, politics, and war was, in fact, probably closer to the human norm than the separation between religion and politics to which we are accustomed. That separation had a distinct historical origin in ancient Sumer, when, in the language of their epic of creation, "kingship came down from the gods" to challenge priestly management of society about 3000 B.C. The rise of kingship in Mesopotamia, as it happens, was also connected with the earliest known manifestation of the tamer version of war dances—close-order drill, encounter with which in its modern form is what started me on this whole inquiry into the muscular aspect of human sociality.

Just as Aztec government existed (at least in theory) to serve the gods and make sure the sun would rise each day by providing Huitzilopochtli with an adequate number of human hearts, so also Sumerian priests affirmed that the gods had created humankind to supply all their material wants through temple offerings. It was the job of priests to organize the necessary human skill and labor to make temple services as splendid as possible and thus please the gods. In return, humanity could hope for divine protection from natural disasters and enemy attacks.

But as the network of canals spread ever further across the flood plains of the Tigris-Euphrates and as wealth accumulated around the temples of the land, barbarian raiding from afar and fighting between adjacent cities over water rights became chronic. As a result, about 3000 B.C., what had begun as temporary military leadership that was renewed for each campaign turned into permanent kingship. The *Epic of Gilgamesh* offers a vivid portrait of the transition. Hero and king, Gilgamesh was both protector and exploiter, whose relations with the citizens of Uruk were as ambiguous as Saul's were with the heads of respectable Hebrew families some two millennia afterwards.[13]

Because priests managed Sumerian written records, along with so much else, Gilgamesh is portrayed as conventionally pious,[14] but it does not take much imagination to realize that resources devoted to warfare had to be subtracted from resources devoted to temple services. Hence, as military enterprise expanded, priestly management of daily activity had to make room for a new rival; and since priests controlled communication with the gods, upstart captains had to rest their power on an entirely secular basis: to wit, on an armed household of followers. Those followers were, I suggest, bound together and, if need be, psychologically prepared to defy both priests and gods, thanks to their collective emotional response to close-order drill.

The *Epic of Gilgamesh* portrays an age when military equipment and manpower still had to be improvised for each campaign,[15] but a few hundred years afterwards royal households comprising large numbers of professional soldiers had become permanent. Moreover, such households fought in close order, and marched in step to maintain an unbroken shield wall against their foes if we judge by a stele, dating from about 2450 B.C., that shows Eannatum, king of Lagash, marching at the head of a body of tightly packed, shield-carrying spearmen. Practice was needed to keep the ranks together, as anyone who has tried to keep step in an academic procession will know; and presumably the *esprit de corps* that modern drill arouses affected Eannatum's soldiers too.

If we assume that the royal house holders spent most of their time in ceremonial guard duty, drill, and military display, it is reasonable to surmise that they resembled well-drilled soldiers of later ages in being largely dissociated from surrounding society by the emotional residues of keeping together in time. It follows that like Louis XIV's soldiers of a later age, they were ready and able to sustain the king's power at home against any and all rivals, whether priestly or popular. A thoroughly secular military system thus took shape in uneasy balance with the sacred priestly power. This remained the case throughout subsequent Mesopotamian history.[16]

Europe, along with all of western and southern Asia, inherited the resulting separation of throne and altar from the Sumerians. China, Japan, and southeast Asia did not; and this continues to be a major divide in the political-religious ordering of society down to our own time.[17] I am tempted to suggest that this (presumed) example of the power of drill to redirect human loyalties was comparably important to Hebrew prophecy in shaping fundamental assumptions among the world's inhabitants today. Merger of religious and military-political forms of power prevailed among the Aztecs, Incas, ancient Egyptians, Chinese, Japanese, southeast Asians, and many other peoples. It was, in fact, the human norm. What happened in Sumer and societies influenced by the civilization of Sumer was exceptional. I suggest that the psychological impact of drill may well have been critical in keeping the military-political structure of ancient Sumer independent of, and sometimes at odds with, priestly-religious authority. If so, this would indeed count as one of the most historically significant manifestations of the effect of muscular bonding in all of human experience.

This is a lot to deduce from a single stele.[18] Secular government might have arisen anyway, without the underpinning of close-order drill. But secular rulership did begin in Sumer, and for a few centuries Sumerian kings did command foot soldiers who marched and fought in close order, armed with spears and protected by shields, as citizen-soldiers of classical Greece were later to do. The case must remain open; and this suggestion arises solely because I am now aware of how powerfully human groups in other situations have responded to the emotions aroused by keeping together in time.

Whether or not it was important for the emergence of secular kingship, close-order drill did not long continue to dominate the battlefields of the ancient Near East. About a century after Eannatum portrayed himself marching at the head of his armored spearmen, a new weapon and new style of warfare, probably introduced by Sargon of Akkad (ca. 2350 B.C.), seems to have made the shield wall obsolete.

Once again, an isolated stele suggests what may have happened. A few decades after Sargon's incessant campaigning had subdued all of Sumer and a wide swathe of other lands surrounding the flood plain, his grandson and successor, Naram Sin, erected a stele showing how he had defeated the inhabitants of distant mountains by ascending the heights and slaying them with his bow. The curve of the bow that Naram Sin carries resembles the shape of compound bows made of wood, sinew, and bone that were used by later generations of steppe warriors. Such bows are far more powerful than bows made only of wood. When first introduced, they probably could penetrate the sort of armor that Sumerian spearmen wore. This made close-ordered troops vulnerable to nimble bowmen, who could attack from a distance and still remain safely beyond the spearmen's reach, and who therefore did not need to wear heavy armor or maintain any fixed formation.

The way Naram Sin's followers straggle below and behind him on his victory stele is compatible with such a view, though it can scarcely be said to prove that close-ordered spearmen had disappeared from Mesopotamian warfare.[19] But later portrayals of battle scenes show troops in open order, often with archer and spearmen paired to combine the offensive capability of long distance missiles with close-in defense. Assyrian and Persian soldiers sometimes marched in step, to judge by the way they appear on palace walls, but nothing resembling the shield wall of Eannatum's time ever showed up again in Mesopotamia or the ancient Near East.[20]

The initial impact of compound bows on infantry tactics was much enlarged when bowmen began using horses to increase their mobility. This, indeed, is what assured the permanent eclipse of unsupported close-ordered spearmen in the Near East and in Eurasia at large. Beginning about 1800 B.C., when horses harnessed to light chariots began to haul bowmen around the battlefield, their strength and fleetness had a devastating effect on less mobile foot soldiers. Then, after about 875 B.C., bowmen dispensed with the encumbrance of chariots by mounting directly on horseback.[21] This was no simple feat. A cavalryman had to aim and shoot while bouncing about on the back of a galloping horse, and simultaneously control his mount without using the hands and arms he needed for bending the bow. But once such skills were mastered, the speed and endurance of horses gave cavalrymen the ability to concentrate superior force at any given spot, almost at will. In open country foot soldiers became easy targets, so that for the ensuing two thousand years cavalry dominated warfare throughout most of Eurasia. Since it is not in the nature of horses to move in unison,[22] drill on the Sumerian model withered away.

Nevertheless, on opposite fringes of the civilized world, infantry drill did reassert itself for a few centuries, both in north China and in the Mediterranean coastlands, with very considerable consequences for subsequent political institutions and ideals. Let me say a few words about each of these cases.

Until near the end of the fourth century B.C., China was insulated from the impact of cavalry. It took a good many centuries for the necessary skills to spread across the steppe from the frontiers of Assyria, where this way of improving mobility in battle presumably originated. Horses and chariots had arrived in China about 1200 B.C. but remained rare and expensive, used as command vehicles in war and for ceremonial hunting.[23] But in the Warring States period, 402–221 B.C., a sharp escalation of military activity occurred, very like what took place in Sumer after 3000 B.C., and results were strikingly similar. Until cavalry changed things, infantry, equipped with what are usually referred to as halberds, dominated battle. Since these weapons could serve either as spears or as battle axes, depending on how they were handled, drill was very necessary to assure that each soldier's movements matched those of his fellows, either holding the spear point steady against the foe, or bringing the axe blade down on his head after lifting the weapon high enough to get sufficient leverage for the blow.

Several ancient texts describe the way Chinese drill masters contrived to avoid entangling the long-handled halberds by making their bearers move precisely and in unison. For example, the most influential military classic, Sun Tzu, *The Art of War,* composed about 400 B.C., tells how he overcame a mocking challenge by training women of the court to use halberds correctly. He got nothing but giggling and laughter at first, but after executing two ringleaders, the text declares: "He repeated the signals on the drums, and the women faced left, right and to the front, to the rear, knelt and rose all in strict accordance with the prescribed drill."[24] Or, again, as an otherwise unidentified author, Wei Liao-tzu, explained about the end of the fourth century B.C.:

> Beat the drum once and the left foot steps forward; beat it again and the right foot advances. . . . If the drummer misses a beat, he is executed. Those that set up a clamor are executed. Those that do not obey the gongs, drums, bells and flags, but move by themselves, are executed. When combat methods are taught to one hundred men, after their instruction is complete, unite them with other companies to comprise one thousand men. When the instruction of one thousand men is complete, unite them with other regiments to comprise ten thousand. When the instruction of the armies of ten thousand is complete, assemble them into the Three Armies. When the masses of the Three Armies can divide and unite, they can execute the methods of large-scale combat. When their instruction is complete, test them with maneuvers.[25]

Such passages show that very large infantry armies were taught to handle their weapons in unison and maintain formation by keeping in step while moving about on the battlefield in response to signals. It sounds very much like eighteenth-century European military training, and we may assume that the psychological impact on Chinese soldiers was much the same as later in Europe. That is to say, well-drilled troops presumably developed their own *esprit de corps*, an unthinking readiness to obey their officers, and an almost complete disregard for competing attachments. In particular, this meant that the old quasi-religious reverence for the imperial Chou dynasty, which still nominally ruled all of China, lost its political effectiveness, while the thoroughly secular power of local sovereigns consolidated itself.

If well-drilled infantry, carrying such a psychological stamp, had remained decisive in battle, China would surely have divided into rival secular states, as Europe did in the early modern period. But instead, new-fangled cavalry (first recorded in 321 B.C.) and the invention of a powerful new missile weapon, the crossbow (first recorded in 341 B.C.),[26] made even the best-drilled infantry excessively vulnerable in the open field. The result was a political-military revolution. Superior access to cavalry and a ruthless concentration of all available resources for war allowed the frontier state of Ch'in to conquer all its rivals by 221 B.C. Thereafter, military and administrative supremacy was again united in the person of the emperor, and after the establishment of the Han dynasty (202 B.C.–220 A.D.), old-fashioned religious authority was deliberately called upon to make the imperial authority august as well as formidable.

Throughout most of China's subsequent history, foot soldiers equipped with crossbows could defend walled cities and other fortified places from raiding horsemen very effectively, but they were too slow and vulnerable to fight in the open field. Hence, despite expressions of reverence for other aspects of Sun Tzu's wisdom, the close-order drill he prescribed became irrelevant to the Chinese style of warfare after about 350 B.C. This remained the case for some nineteen hundred years, until an archaizing general of the sixteenth century discovered how to fight offensive wars, reviving and modifying Sun Tzu's drill while using field fortifications to protect his foot soldiers, even (or especially) in the open steppe.[27]

The real but transitory importance of well-drilled infantry in ancient China was quite exactly matched along the westernmost fringe of civilized society among the ancient Greeks and Romans. Because classical ideas and ideals influenced the world-girdling European political and military practices of recent times, ancient Greece and Rome deserve rather more extended attention here. Keeping time together did prevail for a few centuries in armies and navies manned by Greek and Roman citizens. It follows that the emotional warmth we have learned to expect from such behavior in ancient and hierarchical societies also played its part in establishing active, participatory citizenship that was the hallmark of the Greek and Roman concepts of freedom.

Greek military history has been very thoroughly explored by modern scholars, without however resolving the many uncertainties that envelop the history of the infantry phalanx. Nevertheless, it is clear that from sometime in the seventh century B.C. armored spearmen arrayed in close order dominated Greek battlefields. Spear fighting was not new, if we believe Homer; but whether or not these more tightly arrayed formations transformed politics and gave citizenship new meaning is hotly disputed.

Some facts are clear. In about 675 B.C. a new sort of shield was introduced among the Greeks and spread very rapidly to Italy as well. Hung in the center from the left elbow, with a second handhold near the rim, it allowed its bearers to parry blows effectively. This had not been possible before, when shields were slung around the neck. But the new shields had a corresponding disadvantage: they could not be used to protect the back during retreat. To use them safely, fighting men needed improved protection in flank and rear, and they found it by forming a shield wall like that of ancient Sumer. The resulting phalanx, usually eight ranks deep, could drive less densely arrayed opponents from the field, but only as long as the shield wall remained intact and enemy missiles did not disrupt the formation from a distance.

The conventional practices of classical Greek warfare seem oddly archaic in view of the prominence of cavalry and archery in Persia and Scythia—the two most formidable of Greece's neighbors. But a stubborn preference for spear fighting on foot, evident in Homer, continued to prevail until, starting with episodes of the Peloponnesian War (431–404 B.C.), missile weapons wielded by mercenaries from peripheral lands like Acarnania and Epirus did to the unsupported phalanx what Sargon of Akkad's troops had probably done to Sumerian spearmen almost two thousand years earlier. Subsequently, led by King Philip (d. 336 B.C.) and his son Alexander (d. 323 B.C.), the semi-barbarous Macedonians proved more adept than the Greeks in developing the combined-arms, professionalized style of war that emerged from the encounter between citizen-hoplites (foot soldiers) of Greece and peripheral barbarians in the fourth century B.C.

By comparison with later Macedonian flexibility and complexity, the tactics of hoplite battle seem primitive indeed. Hostile armies had first to find suitable flat ground on which to array themselves before charging headlong. What happened when the front lines met is not sure. Some modern scholars hold that the fighters maintained sufficient distance from one another to permit individual dueling with spear and shield, while others think that pressure from the rear ranks turned battle into a rugby scrum, compressing bodies together and severely cramping anything resembling skilled use of weapons. Battles did not last long, and as soon as one side broke and ran, fighting gave place to rituals for burying the dead, celebrating victory, and mourning defeat.[28]

Phalanx tactics arose when war was a seasonal occupation. Farmers needed to be able to protect their grain fields from raiding neighbors, and they got together in the new massed formation to do so. Two effects followed. First, numbers became critical, since when one phalanx opposed another, the formation with the longer front could assure victory simply by wrapping itself around the enemy's vulnerable flanks and rear. Rival cities therefore had to strive to maximize the number of their hoplites by nurturing as many stalwart farmers as possible. In particular, it became necessary to pass laws to check the consolidation of estates into a few rich men's hands. Reforms associated with the names of Lycurgus in Sparta (ca. 610 B.C.) and of Solon in Athens (594 B.C.) were aimed at achieving this result. Insofar as other Greek cities followed suit, Greek society remained archaic and more nearly egalitarian than would otherwise have been the case.

The second effect of phalanx warfare was that no great differences arose between rural farmers and city folk. This greater homogeneity, too, was archaic by comparison with the alienation between urban rent and tax collectors and rural tax and rent payers that prevailed in the more anciently civilized areas of Egypt and the Middle East. The great advantage was that Greeks could mobilize a larger proportion of their total manpower for war than was possible in countries where differing economic interests divided rich from poor. The corresponding disadvantage was that farmer-citizen-soldiers inevitably had to fight as amateurs.[29]

Yet Athenian amateurs defeated a Persian expeditionary force of experienced soldiers at Marathon in 490 B.C. and, far more surprisingly, the same tactics overcame a truly formidable Persian army at Plataea eleven years later—and did so despite conspicuous disorderliness in the field. The Greek forces comprised contingents from different cities that were unaccustomed to cooperation. As a result, at the critical juncture they actually precipitated Persian attack by conspicuous clumsiness in redeploying on the battlefield.[30] Nonetheless it was the Greeks who won, and their victory allowed them to retain political independence for the next hundred and fifty years and achieve the distinctive expressions of classical civilization we so much admire.

How to account for the surprising outcome of the Persian Wars was problematic at the time—even to the victors, as Herodotus makes clear. It remains so still, but I am not about to address the question anew, wishing merely to ask whether, before and after Plataea, Greek military training had the effect of arousing sentiments of solidarity through keeping together in time.

As far as land warfare is concerned, the answer depends on how hoplites prepared for war and how they learned to keep their places in the phalanx. Surprisingly little is known about these matters. A special institution, the gymnasium, existed to train youths for adult roles, and specifically military exercises were a prominent part of that training. Full-time instructors taught the use of weapons in Athens' three gymnasiums. There young men danced, ran races in full armor, and engaged in other athletic competitions. Aristotle's *Constitution of Athens* says that prospective hoplites enrolled as ephebes at the age of eighteen; after a year in the gymnasium, they paraded before the assembly, where their equipment was inspected and they were formally recognized as qualified for the phalanx. The young men then spent a year of garrison duty on the frontiers before achieving full adult status as citizens and hoplites.[31]

But there is almost no information about military training in the gymnasiums before Aristotle (d. 322 B.C.), and since he does not say anything about collective drill and maneuvers, the question of whether or not Athenian youths prepared individually for participation in the phalanx without serious practice in keeping formation and marching together remains open. Next to nothing is known about what happened in other Greek cities, except for Sparta. Nevertheless, expert opinion holds that "A farmer who was not rich enough to enjoy the leisure necessary for lengthy practice of arms, could, with the minimum of training become competent enough to take his place in the phalanx."[32] And to cite a second opinion: "Drill and exercises in formation seem to have remained at an elementary level," because "for Athenians, in effect, drill could infringe on liberty and personal initiative."[33]

The Spartans, however, did engage in drill and marching exercises and advanced into battle by keeping in step to the sound of music. Two ancient authorities are unambiguous. Thucydides, describing the battle of Mantinea in 418 B.C., says: "After this they joined battle, the Argives and their allies advancing with haste and fury, the Lacedemonians slowly and to the music of many flute players—a standing institution in their army, that has nothing to do with religion, but is meant to make them advance evenly, stepping in time, without breaking their order, as large armies are apt to do in the moment of engaging."[34] Plutarch reports much the same, claiming that Lycurgus had instituted marching in step along with all his other reforms. "It was at once a magnificent and terrible sight," he wrote, "to see them march on to the tune of their flutes, without any disorder in their ranks, any discomposure in their minds, or change in their countenances, calmly and cheerfully moving with music to the deadly fight."[35]

Spartan hoplites also knew how to execute flanking movements, and could close or open ranks so as to alter the length of their front. Some maneuvers apparently required separate files to follow the man in the front rank, thus breaking the phalanx into a tactical unit of just eight men.[36] Prolonged practice was required to assure the smooth execution of such deployments; and, like other Greeks, the Spartans also danced in full panoply, mimicking battle encounters while keeping time to the sound of flutes.[37] Choral songs about how a fighting man ought to conduct himself in battle also figured largely in Spartiate life. Thus song and dance reinforced drill to make the Spartan phalanx what it was.[38]

Hours of marching, dancing, and singing together presumably had the same emotional effects that modern close-order drill does. Accordingly, I feel sure that the warriors of Sparta did indeed experience strong emotional bonding in the classical age. The unique efficiency of the Spartan phalanx resulted; in Athens and other Greek cities, however, occasions for drilling together were probably trivial since, as a leading expert on the subject declares: "Men of military age trained in the gymnasium with little organized supervision."[39]

On the other hand, the Athenian fleet developed muscular bonding among a larger proportion of the total population than ever fought in Sparta's phalanx. In 483 B.C., when Themistocles persuaded the Athenians to build a fleet of triremes, the citizens who manned the oars found themselves in a situation that required prolonged and precise movement in unison. The three tiers of oars had scant clearance. Every oarsman had to keep pace with those in front and behind, while also keeping his oar out of the path of those banked above or below him. Deviation of more than a few inches, and mistiming by a fraction of a second, meant a tangle of oars and loss of momentum. Precision was absolutely vital, and it took considerable practice for a crew to settle into a smooth, effective rhythm.[40]

Rowing flexes the same arm and leg muscles as marching and dancing, and a seated posture may not diminish the emotional effect of keeping together in time that results from such exercises when people stay on their feet. Unlike contemporary rowers, ancient trireme crews pulled their oars in unison by conforming to the beat of a mallet on a special sounding board; and this may have strengthened their visceral response to keeping together in time.[41] If so, the Athenians, too, were in a position to provoke the same sort of emotional solidarity that the Spartans did, with the difference that the upwelling of common feeling among the Athenians concentrated among citizens too poor to equip themselves for the phalanx, and who, instead of fighting on land, rowed in the fleet almost every summer between 480 and 404 B.C.

I suggest, therefore, that the public life of the two cities that did most to define the special character of Greek civilization did indeed derive its extraordinary intensity largely, or perhaps entirely, from the emotional residues of keeping together in time. The strong tie between an individual citizen and the polis (as illustrated for instance by Socrates' life and death) and the encroachment on private life that citizenship entailed (especially among the Spartans) can scarcely be explained otherwise. More importantly, feelings aroused by moving together in unison undergirded the ideals of freedom and equality under law that characterized both Athens and Sparta. The muscular basis of such sentiments also explains why the rights of free and equal citizens were limited to the militarily active segment of the population. Those who moved together, whether on land or or sea, were also those who assembled together to deliberate about war and peace and other matters of state—and paid the price by acting on their decisions afterwards.

The ideal of free, participatory citizenship as thus defined among the Greeks in the fifth century B.C. echoes among us today almost as loudly as do the pronouncements of the Hebrew prophets. That is because the Greek political ideal achieved persuasive expression in the works of historians, dramatists, and philosophers. Once again, practices that had emerged (at least in part) from keeping time together achieved lasting influence when translated into words and transmitted to subsequent generations in literary dress. But without being rooted in the experience of keeping together in time, I suggest that Greek notions of political freedom and equality could not have blossomed so enduringly in practice or been expressed so eloquently as in fact they were.

To be sure, Greek citizens did not long submit willingly to the rigors of military drill and rowing, but the emotional effects of keeping together in time did not disappear from the classical world when citizen soldiers and rowers ceased to dominate military affairs. Quite the contrary, drill became more elaborate and prolonged; but the soldiers who drilled were professionals whose loyalties were to their commanders rather than to the polis (or the kingdom) as a whole, and only in exceptional circumstances did they take any further part in political decision-making.

Little is known for sure. The Athenian general Iphicrates (d. ca. 348 B.C.) became famous for keeping his mercenary troops from idleness by drilling them incessantly and finding other kinds of work for them to do.[42] King Philip of Macedon (d. 336 B.C.) did the same, and made his soldiers carry two-and-a-half days' supplies of everything they needed, thereby achieving an unparalleled rapidity of march. The only surviving text that purports to describe Macedonian drill dates from the second century A.D., when Roman armies were about to follow Alexander's example by heading eastward into Mesopotamia. It is a short treatise, written in Greek and dedicated to Hadrian by an otherwise unknown writer, Aelianus Tacticus. It smacks of the lamp, not of the drill field, describing intricate geometrical patterns of march and deployment that look tidier on paper than likely in practice.[43] Still, there is every reason to suppose that close-order infantry drill was practiced regularly by Macedonian armies, since handling their elongated spears without tangling them up was as tricky (and as necessary) as keeping Chinese halberds straight had been a few decades before.[44]

Soldiers shaped by service in the Macedonian armies of Philip, Alexander, and their successors were entirely detached from citizenship. Instead, they followed their commanders, who in turn (at least usually) obeyed the king. This in effect assimilated Hellenistic military arrangements to the bureaucratic imperial pattern that had prevailed in the Middle East ever since Sargon of Akkad's time, whereby an armed ethnic minority, supported by taxes wrung from reluctant subjects, defended the land (more or less effectually) against rival and perhaps more ruthless plunderers.

In such a system of government the resulting gap between military specialists and the taxpaying public was, of course, enormous. In contrast, the Greek cities at their apogee expected every full citizen to participate personally in military campaigns to protect the farmland that fed the community. This simplicity disappeared from the Hellenic world with the rapid professionalization of warfare after 404 B.C. But off to the west in Italy, the Romans recapitulated the Greek experience, lagging behind by almost four centuries in converting citizen soldiers of the early Republic into a bureaucratic professional army.

In the days of the Republic it was Rome's citizen soldiers who conquered Italy. But how they acquired the necessary skills for deploying in battle is simply not explained by surviving texts. Almost everything that is known or surmised on the subject comes from a tract written sometime in the fourth or perhaps even in the fifth century A.D. by an author about whom nothing is known but his name, Flavius Renatus Vegetius.[45]

If Vegetius is to be believed—and since he was probably writing in the hope of reforming practices of his own day, he may have exaggerated the rigor of the training Roman soldiers had once experienced—drill in formation was very much a part of Roman military practice. In his words: "At the beginning of the training, the recruit must be taught the military pace. . . . This can only be achieved if, by continuous practice, they learn to march quickly and in time."[46] He goes on to declare that twenty miles a day was standard for cross-country marching, and prescribes field exercises thrice a month for garrison troops, whereby they were supposed to march ten miles into open country, build a fortified camp, and return to their base, all in a single day.[47] Individual skill with weapons was developed by systematic daily practice, using swords to attack wooden posts set in the drill ground to simulate enemy soldiers.

Although much of what Vegetius prescribes may have actually prevailed at one time or another, his account presupposes a fully professional soldiery living in regular cantonments with nothing to do but train for future battles. That does not fit republican reality, and it seems improbable that such relentless training was ever pursued for long periods of time, and certainly not before Augustus dispatched the legions to the frontiers after 27 B.C.[48] Yet for all the uncertainties about the history of Roman methods of training, it seems probable that as they clashed with Carthaginian and Hellenistic armies, the Romans learned to employ the same sorts of drill that had developed among those thoroughly professionalized troops.[49]

We may accept enough of what Vegetius says to believe that drill became systematic under the empire. Resulting *esprit de corps* and emotional bonding within the ranks presumably helped to sustain the army's efficiency and obedience until the third century A.D. Thus the long Roman peace, as well as the disruption of the Republic that preceded it, were rooted in the emotional residues of military drill as much or more than in Stoic ideas, landowners' interests, or the decay of republican virtue and moral exhaustion after the brutal civil wars.

Like all things human, the Roman peace did not last. The legions that had sustained it lost their military efficiency, partly for economic, demographic, and social reasons, and partly because a new style of armored heavy cavalry, equipped with powerful compound bows, put even well-trained Roman foot soldiers at a serious disadvantage.[50] The upshot in the West was the eventual collapse of imperial government, while emperors in the East carried through a (precariously) successful military reorganization by putting their principal effort into creating an imperial field army of mounted archers, or cataphracts.[51] The eclipse of infantry in the eastern Roman or Byzantine empire by the time of Justinian (527–565 A.D.) was not matched in the more backward West until after the collapse of the Carolingians in the ninth century. Thereafter, mounted warriors asserted their primacy in France and Germany also, spreading to adjacent parts of western Christendom in the ensuing century and inaugurating a cavalry age that lasted until the fourteenth century.[52]

Such changes merely assimilated the warfare of the Far West to styles of combat prevailing throughout the rest of Eurasia. As we saw, Chinese warfare had been transformed by the onrush of cavalry from about 350 B.C. Cavalrymen also prevailed in the Middle East, India, Japan, and throughout the Eurasian steppelands; and wherever cavalry bowshot dominated battlefields, close-order drill and the emotional effects it produces became trivial or were entirely obliterated.[53]

Even when mounted knights ruled European battlefields, foot soldiers undoubtedly outnumbered them, since each knight needed servants and supporters to keep himself, his horse, and his weapons in working order. But infantrymen whose role was to support (and mop up after) a cavalry charge remained subordinate. Warfare in western Europe began to alter when drilled infantry, whether independent or in rivalry with mounted knights, regained importance. This started as early as the twelfth century, when Italian townsmen managed to defeat an imperial army of German knights that recklessly charged the close-arrayed burghers' pikes at Legnano in 1176. A bit more than a century later, Swiss infantry repelled the knights that their Hapsburg overlord sent to subdue them and soon established themselves as the most formidable pikemen of Europe. Oddly enough, in distant Japan pikemen also proved their usefulness against charging cavalry, beginning in the fourteenth century;[54] while in the Middle East Ottoman foot soldiers, the famous Janissaries, started winning victories for the sultans in the fifteenth century; and offensive deployment of infantry changed the Chinese way of war in the sixteenth. Except in Europe, pikemen succeeded in battle only in association with cavalry bowmen, who guarded the flanks, harassed the enemy with their missiles, and were ready to pursue the fleeing foe as soon as charging pikes broke up the opposing army. In Europe cavalry continued to prefer the lance; and light infantry equipped with crossbows (or in England with long bows) provided pikemen with long range missile support, while knightly cavalry defended flanks and rear.

Wherever massed pikemen began to take part in battle, we can assume that practice was needed to keep formation; marching in step was the obvious way to achieve that result. All the same, as far as my reading goes, there seems to be next to no information available about close-order drill until the reforms associated with the names of Ch'i Chi-kuang in China (d. 1587) and Maurice of Nassau, Prince of Orange, in Europe (d. 1625). Let me therefore skip over the centuries during which infantry formations gradually regained decisive importance in battle, and focus briefly on these two figures.

Ch'i Chi-kuang was a Chinese general whose reforms of the Ming army's training and deployment on the northwest frontier gave the Chinese a new offensive capability on the open steppes, allowing them in the next two centuries to conquer the nomad peoples of the eastern half of Asia and thus create the imperial China we know today.

The secret of Ch'i's success was twofold. On the one hand, he took Sun Tzu's remarks about drill, more drill, and still more drill at face value, as Chinese military men had ceased to do after the fourth century B.C., when cavalry archers made close-order infantry formations excessively vulnerable in the open field. Ch'i overcame that difficulty with a simple technical innovation: when enemy attack threatened, he formed protective lagers out of light and heavy carts that carried baggage and supplies.[55] Unit drill correspondingly expanded to include carefully worked out patterns of deployment, whereby marching men could shift from column to lager and back again at a moment's notice. Wagon lagers protected the infantry's flanks and rear from nomad cavalrymen's arrows; and by leaving portals in the wall of wagons, Chinese cavalry and infantry forces could sally forth whenever a favorable opportunity offered for going over to the offensive. Such tactics allowed well-trained troops to march across the grasslands secure from devastating surprise. This in turn allowed Chinese armies to break up state structures on the steppes by destroying nomad headquarters, harassing the herds, and depriving men and animals of safe and sure refuge.

In effect, being able to move at will across the grasslands meant that Chinese numbers could now be brought to bear against the nomads' superior mobility as never before. The age-old standoff between steppe horsemen and Chinese settlers was thereby permanently upset. Mounted herdsmen could no longer effectively resist Chinese military power, even though it was not until 1757 that the last autonomous nomad confederacy was destroyed, when Kalmuks, fleeing from their Chinese enemy, had to seek Russian protection.

In 1568, Ch'i experimented with his new style of field operations by organizing what can best be called a "cart division." As eventually standardized, such divisions comprised 126 heavy carts, 216 light carts, 3,000 cavalry, and 11,000 infantry; and thanks to the carts' carrying capacity, his foot soldiers had access both to halberds for close-in defense and to crossbows for the attack. This pattern of troop organization soon proved its practical value, combining mobility with security in the open field. By 1574, when Ch'i was promoted to the topmost rank of the Chinese army and took up his new post at Peking, he had sixteen cart divisions with a nominal strength of 224,000 men under his command. His divisions routinely practiced maneuvers on a scale surpassing anything European armies attempted before the nineteenth century. And at the individual and small-unit level, everyday training involved endless drill in use of weapons and deployment, from march to lager and back again, so that in principle and to a large degree also in practice, each man knew his assigned task and station in every foreseeable tactical circumstance.

Ch'i's achievements were appreciated by the court, as a citation issued by the Ministry of War on the occasion of his promotion to supreme command aptly demonstrates: "In a hundred battles," it says, "Ch'i has shown a brave heart. He has completely mastered the victory calculations of Sun Tzu. He understands the established rules of the ancients, and he understands their implementation."[56] He followed his successes on the northwest frontier by organizing comparably mobile forces to oppose Japanese pirates who had been raiding the coasts of China, meeting with considerable success on that front, too, before his retirement in 1582.

Indeed, Ch'i's combination of old and new fitted Chinese needs so well that it became normative thereafter. His fame and influence were much magnified by the fact that he explained in detail what needed to be done by writing two books, entitled *A New Treatise on Disciplined Service* (1560) and *A Practical Account of Troop Training* (1571). They were frequently republished thereafter, most recently in 1939, because Chiang Kai-shek wanted his troops to have the benefit of Ch'i's instruction. Ch'i's books were also translated into Korean in 1787 and into Japanese in 1798.

The Manchus, who established the Ching dynasty in 1644, changed Chinese military arrangements by planting garrisons of Manchu cavalrymen—so-called Banners—at strategic points in China proper; and, being less hostile to the Mongols than the Ming had been, they also enrolled Mongol cavalrymen in some of their Banners. By combining these traditional cavalry forces with Ch'i's style of combined arms, the Manchus were able to expand their power across China's traditional borders, occupying Tibet, pacifying Mongolia, and in 1755 destroying the last formidable steppe confederation, which had been organized by a people known as Jungars. The empire that we call China thus came into existence in the course of the eighteenth century.

By 1839–1841, when European troops first clashed with Chinese soldiers, the rigor of Ch'i's training was much reduced and internal unrest had already begun to threaten the dynasty. Moreover, by that time the effectiveness of European weapons had far outstripped anything the Chinese had at their disposal. As a result, even small European forces had no great difficulty in penetrating Chinese coastal defenses. Thereafter, western-ers' disdain for Chinese military traditions prevented them from recognizing how Ch'i's archaizing reforms had succeeded in upsetting the millennial balance between nomad mobility and Chinese numbers that had kept the Chinese at a disadvan-tage ever since 350 B.C.

Disregard of China's military achievements was increased by the fact that Ch'i's reforms had entirely neglected the offensive capability of handguns. This made sense at the time, for the crossbows his infantry used were far cheaper and more effec-tive against unarmored nomad cavalry than the clumsy hand-guns of the age. China had pioneered the development of gunpowder weapons, beginning about 1000,[57] but found far less use for them than Europeans did. In particular, the Chinese had no reason to build cannon to knock down the walls they were trying to defend; and their crossbows were so much cheaper and quicker-firing than early handguns that they had no inducement to develop infantry gunpowder weapons either. They did develop medium caliber guns for protecting ships and harbors, but were left far behind by the reckless way that Europeans, from the fourteenth century onwards, began to invest in gunpowder weaponry of every size, from monstrous bombards to hand-held pistols.

This cost the Chinese dear after 1839, but ought not to detract from our appreciation of the success with which Ch'i Chi-kuang wedded archaizing reform with cost-effective tech-nological innovation in the sixteenth century. His military reforms helped the Chinese, in tandem with the Russians, to extinguish the political-military power of the Eurasian steppe nomads forever; they made China what it is today, the world's only surviving imperial state. Few individuals in the entire history of the world can boast of such a conspicuous monument.

R USSIAN EXPANSION across Asia also rested on military reforms initiated about a generation later and at the other extreme of Eurasia by Maurice of Orange, Captain General of Holland from 1585 until his death in 1625. Like Ch'i Chi-kuang, Maurice also made a deliberate effort to return to ancient models of infantry training, but of course looked to the Greeks and Romans rather than to the pages of Sun Tzu's *Art of War*. In addition, Maurice's style of drill was propagated throughout Christian Europe by means of a book that illustrated every move in full detail. These coincidences with General Ch'i's career are impressive; all the more so when one recognizes that both Ch'i and Maurice succeeded in making infantry the queen of battles, within a system of combined arms, by inadvertently tapping the inherent human emotional response to keeping together in time. Both in the Far East and Far West, prolonged drill created obedient, reliable, and effective soldiers, with an *esprit de corps* that superseded previous identities and insulated them from outside attachments. Well-drilled new-model soldiers, whether Chinese or European, could therefore be counted on to obey their officers accurately and predictably, even when fighting hundreds or thousands of miles away from home. The Chinese and all modern European empires were built on the strength of this remarkable behavior.

When Maurice of Orange succeeded to his murdered father's command over Dutch troops in 1585, he inherited a war with Spain. Spanish soldiers, having driven the French out of Italy in 1559 after half a century of intermittent war, then stood at the apex of their power and prestige. As befitted a university man with an up-to-date humanistic education, Maurice looked to the ancients for guidance when he set out to improve the performance of the troops under his command.[58] This archaizing bent took him directly to the pages of two ancient archaizers, Aelianus and Vegetius, whom we have previously met. At the time, Aelianus was newly translated into Latin, so that for Maurice the elaborate geometrical drill he prescribed combined the attraction of novelty with the prestige of antiquity. Yet simple replication of Macedonian methods of training was out of the question. Gunpowder weapons had changed European warfare in ways undreamed of in antiquity, so Maurice and his collaborators had to adapt ancient principles to radically new circumstances. They did so with distinguished success.[59]

From Aelianus their key borrowing was the simple notion of training soldiers to move simultaneously in response to stylized "words of command." Aelianus had listed twenty-two different "words of command" used by the Macedonians; but by the time Maurice's cousin and aide, Johann of Nassau, had analyzed the motions required to handle a matchlock, he counted forty-two distinct postures, and assigned a fixed word of command to each of them. A simpler drill, far closer to Macedonian precedents, was also devised for pikemen, who were needed to protect the arquebusiers from cavalry attack during the rather lengthy process of reloading.

The practical importance of such pedantry was very great. In principle and to a surprising degree also in practice, it became possible to get soldiers to move in unison while performing each of the actions needed to load, aim, and fire their guns. The resulting volleys came faster, and misfires were fewer when everyone acted in unison and kept time to shouted commands. Practice and more practice, repeated endlessly whenever spare time allowed, made the necessary motions almost automatic and less likely to be disrupted by stress of battle.[60] More lead projected at the enemy in less time was the result: a definite and obvious advantage when meeting troops not similarly trained. This was what Maurice and his drill masters had aimed for; and once their success became clear, the technique spread to other European armies with quite extraordinary rapidity.

Maurice did not try to keep his methods secret. To allow his soldiers and drill masters to learn the required motions exactly, Johann of Nassau commissioned an accomplished artist, Jacob de Gheyn, to make engravings of each posture required by the new drill, with the corresponding word of command printed beneath each picture. These proved so useful that they were gathered together into a book and published with a brief explanatory text in 1607.[61] A German translation using the same plates came out in 1614, and a Russian version followed in 1649. As these books became available, innumerable drill sergeants, simply by looking at the pictures and memorizing the appropriate words of command, were able to replicate Prince Maurice's drill throughout Europe, and did so within a few decades. Even the Spanish were persuaded to remodel their methods of military training when French troops, instructed in the new fashion, defeated them at Rocroi in 1643.

Maurice made two other notable changes in army management based, however, on Roman rather than Macedonian precedents. According to Vegetius and other authorities (not least, Julius Caesar), whenever Roman soldiers made camp, they erected temporary fortifications to guard against surprise. Accordingly, Maurice required his soldiers to construct fortifications in the field, digging trenches and raising earthen embankments to protect them from enemy fire. Burrowing in the ground may not have been heroic, but it was effective in preserving lives; and since most field operations in the Dutch wars (1567–1609) turned into sieges, digging dominated active campaigning just as drill did when troops were in garrison or, exceptionally, fought a battle in the open.

Idleness, in effect, was banished from military life. This was a great departure from earlier custom, since waiting for something to happen occupies almost all of a soldier's time, and when left to their own devices, troops had traditionally escaped boredom by indulging in drink and other sorts of dissipation. Debauchery was not banished entirely under the regime Prince Maurice and his imitators established, but it was usually confined to off-duty leave time. Soldiers who had been well exercised by digging and drilling during the day could be counted on to go peaceably to sleep at night, so that armies became much more comfortable neighbors for civilians than ever before.

In addition, Maurice adjusted the size of tactical units so that even the largest, a battalion of 440 men, could respond to a single commander's voice. Companies, platoons, and squads, each responsive to its designated leader, completed the chain of command. Regular formations of march and deployment had long been customary in European armies. What Maurice did differently was to establish prescribed commands for standard maneuvers of units of every size, and then required his troops to practice them whenever there was no digging to be done or drill masters tired of the manual of arms.

When an entire army had been trained in this fashion, far more effective control of the course of battle became possible. Relatively precise coordination between different units and adjustment to unexpected circumstances became quicker and more predictable. Such an army, in effect, had the advantages of a central nervous system. Everything went faster. Obedience was more nearly automatic. The commander's intention and actual performance converged as never before. As a result, victories over less well-trained opponents could be counted on. And since, beyond the circle of European states, the armed elites of other civilizations remained loyal to their own traditions and refused to imitate the new European drill—in most cases until the nineteenth century—European armies acquired a superiority they had not enjoyed before. The history of the ensuing three hundred years reflected this growing imbalance, as more and more dependable military force became cheaply available to European states for the protection of their trade and settlements throughout the rest of the world.

The sociological and psychological side-effects of military drill as developed by Prince Maurice and his imitators were probably just as important as the advantages conferred on European armies in battle. Prolonged drill allowed soldiers, recruited from the fringes of an increasingly commercialized society—individuals for whom the cunning and constraint of the marketplace were repugnant and unworkable—to create a new, artificial primary community among themselves, where comradeship prevailed in good times and bad and where old-fashioned principles of command and subordination gave meaning and direction to life. Men who had little else to be proud of could share an *esprit de corps* with their fellows and glory in their collective sufferings and prowess.

Surrendering personal will to the command of another, while simultaneously merging mindlessly into a group of fellow subordinates, liberates the individual concerned from the burden of making choices.[62] Many young men, especially the poor and propertyless, finding it hard to achieve satisfactory adult roles in an increasingly commercial society, solved their problem by enlisting as soldiers. Hence, as long as food and a pittance of pay were regularly forthcoming, recruiting was seldom difficult. Able-bodied members of the "dangerous classes"—men of whom the Duke of Wellington is reputed to have said, "I don't know what effect these men will have on the enemy, but, by God, they frighten me"[63]—were swiftly and reliably transformed into pillars of the establishment.

This sleight of hand was not miraculous, though it remains surprising. Experience showed that drill quickly made men into soldiers for whom ties beyond the circle of their fellows faded to insignificance. From the point of view of rulers and the propertied classes, it therefore became perfectly safe to give lethal weapons to drifters from city streets and to poor peasant boys. Becoming a soldier turned a recruit "into another man," as Samuel said to Saul about joining the prophets,[64] and in both cases, I suggest, what made the difference was keeping time together and responding to the primal upwelling of collective solidarity that such behavior aroused.

No one understood this at the time, though innumerable soldiers surely felt it from the start and behaved accordingly. Men born to poverty obeyed their superiors without question, even when, as occasionally happened, this required them to shoot rebellious peasants or rioting city crowds.[65] And as a matter of course, men who had no obvious stake in the outcome, and did have very obvious private reasons for wishing to get out of the path of enemy bullets, nonetheless risked their lives in innumerable battles, deploying and firing their weapons as commanded to do, even when sent to fight in distant, alien lands.

We are used to such extraordinary behavior, but that makes it no less strange. It was only possible because, behind and beneath the goals and glories that explained and justified European wars, lurked the primitive solidarity of muscular bonding. Fear of punishment, though real enough in Old Regime armies, was a pale second to the positive force of the shared emotional identity that routinely, naturally, inevitably prevailed among well-drilled troops.

THE CONSEQUENCES of systematic drill for European society were much enhanced by another kind of muscular exertion that simultaneously altered the behavior of the topmost nobility. Courtly dancing took new and self-conscious forms in Italy during the Renaissance, and by the sixteenth century efforts to introduce Italian sophistication into trans-Alpine Europe produced a series of manuals about how to dance in the new styles.[66] An obscure English poet of the sixteenth century, Sir

John Davies, expressed the significance of such performances
aptly when he wrote:

> Concord's true picture shineth in this art
> Where diverse men and women rankèd be
> And everyone does dance a several part,
> Yet all as one in measure do agree,
> Observing perfect uniformity.
> All turn together, all together trace
> And all together honour and embrace.[67]

But it was in the next century, at the French court of Louis
XIV (r. 1648–1715), that dancing and associated courtly rituals achieved their classical expression. As a boy Louis survived
an aristocratic uprising, the so-called Fronde (1648–1653).
After taking power in his own right, he deliberately set out
to prevent recurrence of such unruly behavior. His first line
of defense was to maintain a well-drilled standing army, per-
petually at the ready to nip revolt in the bud. With the help
of his notorious drill-master, Inspector General of Infantry
Col. Jean Martinet, Louis soon made his army the most famed
and feared in Europe. But a second tactic was no less effective:
to wit, the king's requirement that powerful French noblemen
live at his court for long periods of time. There they took
part in continual rituals, dances, formal levées, military displays, and the like, both passively as spectators and actively
as participants.

Louis was a talented dancer. In his youth he practiced every
day, preparing for the leading role (which was always his) in
ballet performances that were presented before the assembled
courtiers on festive occasions. He expected them to take dancing seriously, even after he, at age twenty six, withdrew from
so strenuous a way of demonstrating his personal prowess.
Thereafter professional dancers took over, developing what we
know as classical ballet. But the king continued to take part in
ballroom dances and expected his courtiers to do the same.[68]

Music and costume enhanced the emotional impact of ballet and ballroom dances, and the same may be said of the progresses, formal receptions, and other routines with which Louis filled his day. Courtiers' assigned roles were as artificial as those of the dancers in the ballet, shaped by their place in an ever-changing constellation of personalities, all carefully marshaled around the king's person. Manners became a mask; and the mask of manners, expressed in speech and bodily movements, altered the French high nobility by changing the way they felt about themselves, about each other, and about the king.[69]

The resulting change of aristocratic behavior was intimately connected with the change of soldiers' lives that occurred at the same time. Nearly all of the officers of Louis's new standing army were French noblemen, usually of lower rank than the courtiers. Military march-pasts and maneuvers were very much part of the rituals of the court; and their effect, like that of courtly dances and levées, was to make the aristocracy more peaceful at home and far more obedient to the royal will than ever before.

Louis' deliberate reordering of military and court routines enhanced a feedback loop that had been fitfully advancing in Europe since the tenth century. Under his regime, radically improved civil peace allowed his subjects to increase their wealth, making tax collection easier; an enhanced tax income, in turn, allowed Louis to pay for his court and army, conquer new territories, and make himself and France a model for the rest of Europe.[70]

The Old Regime that took shape as other European states began to imitate (and resist) the French was the era in which European military and political power clearly outstripped that of other peoples. To be sure, Europeans had already overwhelmed Amerindian societies, beginning with the first contacts in 1492; but colonization of the Americas depended less on military than on epidemiological superiority, since the lethal diseases imported from the Old World were what disrupted Amerindian societies, not the conquistadores' ill-organized and poorly equipped military expeditions.[71] By the eighteenth century, however, the routines of European military administration and practice had left other armed establishments far behind.

This became particularly evident in India, where first the French and next the English trained local soldiers in the European manner and then, by intervening in local disputes, swiftly emerged as arbiters and *de facto* rulers of the land. The decisive tip point came during the Seven Years' War (1756–1763), when the British navy assisted the East India Company's soldiers in driving out the French, conquering Bengal, and establishing British predominance throughout most of the rest of India. Indian soldiers trained in the European fashion won these remarkable victories under British leadership. Clearly, what made them such useful and obedient servants of an alien power was the effect of drill in creating among them an *esprit de corps* that overrode competing identities and loyalties.[72]

But as British empire in India began to emerge from the global struggle of the Seven Years' War, their simultaneous success in driving the French from Canada had the effect of detaching the American colonies from any residual dependence on Great Britain. Old and new frictions soon provoked revolt, and, with help from France, the United States of America won its independence in 1783 after a long and difficult war.

The military events in North America had unusual political importance, because the republican principles proclaimed from Philadelphia in 1776 blatantly challenged European monarchy and social hierarchy with an ideal of active, egalitarian citizenship that harked back to the freedom and equality of ancient Rome and Greece. The republican contagion soon spread to France; and in the heat of the subsequent revolutionary wars (1792–1799) new patterns of social mobilization found unprecedented scope.

As we saw in the chapter on small communities, the French revolutionaries experimented with Liberty tree dances and civic festivals that gave muscular public expression to the revolutionary principles of liberty, equality, and fraternity. Larger numbers of citizens were more permanently affected by the *levée en masse,* proclaimed in 1793, which made all adult males liable to military service. Hitherto unmatched numbers of Frenchmen were swiftly drafted into the republican armies, and hurried into battle with minimal training. The victories that ensued rested more on *élan* and numbers than on disciplined tactics, though artillery specialists and other military experts inherited from the royal army of the Old Regime also played an important part.[73] But as year after year of warfare continued, the French armies recapitulated the path Roman armies had taken. The revolutionary soldiers ceased to be self-conscious citizens and became professionals, with loyalties attached to their commanders rather than to the Republic. Napoleon took advantage of this transformation to bestride Europe after 1799, until his foes, having gone at least half way towards mobilizing their peoples on the French model, succeeded in defeating him in 1814 and again in 1815.

Thereafter, European governments were wary of too much popular participation in government. Yet the revolutionary ideal of a free and equal citizenry, exercising rightful sovereignty over the nation as a whole through elected representatives, could not be banished from European politics completely, despite repressive police and sporadic efforts at thought control. The reason for its persistence was that constituted authorities were halfhearted in attacking the revolutionary heritage, because both victors and vanquished recognized that taking the people into more active partnership was the secret of enhancing state power. This had been convincingly demonstrated by French revolutionaries as well as by their foes, and no one wished to undo it entirely.

Muscular embodiment of new notions of citizenship found its most significant expression after the Prussians met humiliating defeat at the battle of Jena in 1806. Germany's subsequent subjugation by the French gave special urgency to the cultivation of bodily excellence in preparation for future resistance. Friedrich Ludwig Jahn (1778–1852) responded by organizing gymnastic clubs, starting at Berlin in 1811. The Turners, to give them their German name, met two or three times a week and soon attracted restless young men who sang patriotic songs, marched, and flexed their muscles in conspicuous ways in the open spaces of many German towns. Preparation for military service against the French was always in the background of their public exhibitions of gymnastic strength and skill, and when the Prussian government actually called on its people to rise against Napoleon in 1813, the Turners rushed to volunteer. But after the war the government prohibited their clubs in 1820, on the ground that they were propagating subversive ideals of German nationalism and liberalism. Prussia legalized the Turners again in 1842, and they played a small, enthusiastic role in the Revolution of 1848. After it failed, refugees transferred gymnastics to the United States, and the Turners of St. Louis, Cincinnati, and Louisville also played a small but strategic role in the American Civil War.[74]

Gymnastics in the Turner mold thereafter developed into the Olympic sport we know today, repeating the path by which ballet had shifted from participatory activity to public spectacle at Louis XIV's court. But in Sweden gymnastics took a different, more popular and far more influential turn. The distinctive Swedish tradition started when Per Heinrich Ling established a Central Institute for Gymnastics at Stockholm in 1814. He classified bodily exercises as medical, military, and aesthetic, devising suitable forms for each. Subsequently, his son and successor Hjalmar Friedrich Ling (1820–1886) devised exercises specifically for schools. They required no special equipment, allowing large numbers to participate at negligible cost.

What we know as calisthenics thus emerged in the 1840s and soon spread far and wide. The basic idea was simplicity itself. An instructor demonstrated an exercise so all could see him or her (for calisthenics became something of a female speciality in Great Britain and some other countries), and then everyone was expected to perform the same motions, often in time to music or simply "by the numbers" as called out by the leader. As the word "calisthenics" implies, fluidity, grace, and muscular precision were the aims; mass movement in unison was the means; and all the emotional responses we have learned to expect from such behavior began to flow from such performances, whenever they were experienced with suitable frequency and duration. Meanings attached to the emotions aroused by calisthenics differed with circumstances, but in most of the world calisthenics came to be closely associated with the cultivation of national solidarity.

Calisthenic exercises in which scores, hundreds, or thousands of schoolchildren took part, quickly spread to most European countries and were also taken up with particular enthusiasm in Japan and China. Exact paths of transmission varied from case to case, and instructors constantly elaborated explanations of what they were trying to accomplish. Thus in Prussia, for example, Swedish patterns had to adjust to pre-existing German and Swiss traditions of physical training. Calisthenics entered the Prussian schools starting in 1846, when an enthusiastic artillery officer brought Swedish methods to official attention. The Ministry of Education made Swedish gymnastics compulsory in all elementary schools in 1862 and extended the practice to secondary schools three years later. Gymnastics also became part of army training, and a single institution, set up in 1851, prepared instructors for both until separate training institutes were established in 1877. Since Prussian authorities viewed physical training in schools as propaedeutic to military

service, official manuals for gymnastics teachers always emphasized the military benefits to be derived from accurate and
obedient execution of commands.[75]

By way of contrast, Swedish gymnastics entered England as
a form of medical therapy and only gained a foothold in
schools after 1877, when the London School Board hired a
Swedish woman to teach gymnastics to girls. She met with such
success that her system was soon extended to boys and spread
widely among state-supported institutions. For the upper
classes, however, a tradition of team sports continued to prevail in the so-called public schools. Prescribed mass exercises
therefore became the hallmark of the less privileged members
of society until, in the twentieth century, games and the requi-
site playing fields also became generally available in state-supported schools.

The British initially made no connection between gymnastics
and national excellence or military service. But in the last
decade of the nineteenth century, when Great Britain began to
feel threatened by Germany, a conscious effort to imitate the
Germans by nationalizing and militarizing physical training
got under way. In particular, voluntary military drill became
widespread in schools, and Empire Day, observed on Queen
Victoria's birthday (May 24), became a school holiday
throughout the British empire. It was celebrated with marching, calisthenics, and song, as well as with appropriately patriotic speeches. These ceremonies were abandoned after World
War II, having been much contaminated, at least in Canada,
by fireworks displays and other motifs borrowed from the
celebration of July Fourth in the United States.[76]

Like the British, Americans kept gymnastics and patriotism
apart when the Swedish model of physical education crossed the
ocean. Indeed, the Young Men's Christian Association (like the
Boy Scouts an import from Britain) became the principal initial
vehicle for propagating Swedish gymnastics in America, and
YMCA missionaries from the United States subsequently played

the same role in China. But calisthenics did not remain immured in YMCA gyms for very long. Instead, American schoolchildren and soldiers were quickly introduced to these exercises, though, thanks perhaps to their transmission via the YMCA, American calisthenics generated rather less patriotic fervor than prevailed in Germany and the Slavic countries of Europe.

Gymnastics became the dominant way of cultivating national consciousness in the Czech lands, where Sokol societies, established in imitation of the German Turners, developed an acute awareness of Czechs' separate identity. Founded in Prague in 1862, the Sokol soon created a network of branches that became the principal vehicle of Czech national consciousness thereafter. More than any other people of Europe, the Czechs built their nation around the cultivation of athletic prowess. Their national cult of bodily excellence rested on a base of mass calisthenics, conducted by privately organized societies where both Swedish and Turner exercises were pursued. Other Slavic nations followed suit, so that by 1912 an All-Slavic Gymnastic Meet could be staged in Prague with no fewer than 20,000 participants.[77]

The French, on the other hand, resisted the German model even after 1870, when a few gymnastic societies were indeed established on French soil with explicitly patriotic intent. But French national feeling fitted awkwardly into the Swedish-German style of muscular *Gleichshaltung*. Schools continued to disdain athletic prowess, and when sports finally arrived in France, the French opted for bicycle racing, which became popular in the 1890s. Other games followed—tennis, rowing, and the like—in the English, upper-class amateur mode. Gymnastics and organized mass exercises never took root.[78]

These and other variations among the different nations of Europe arose as cheap, easily transmitted Swedish-German mass exercises impinged on local institutions and attitudes. Beyond the circle of European nations, the same mix of old and new prevailed, with the difference that what had been chronologically separate waves of muscular bonding in Europe—first close-order drill for soldiers, then calisthenics for civilians and schoolchildren—often coincided in time and won acceptance as aspects of a single effort at self-strengthening intended to catch up with western nations. This was conspicuously the case in the Far East, where odd and unexpected resonances between traditional muscular expression of Buddhist sectarian dissent, on the one hand, and European drill and gymnastics, on the other, allowed old and new forms of muscular bonding to interact in strange and remarkable ways.

Before sketching what happened in Japan and China, however, it is instructive to compare their (eventually) enthusiastic response with the mixed reception of European drill and calisthenics in the Islamic world. In India, well-drilled soldiers, both Moslem and Hindu, continued to serve reliably throughout the nineteenth century, with one conspicuous exception, when British disregard of religious taboos triggered an unexpected mutiny in 1857–58. Thereafter, the British were careful to observe religious sensibilities and brigaded Indian and British units together more systematically than before. Despite the mutiny, the government in London continued to find it safe and convenient to rely very largely on Indian manpower for numerous colonial wars in Asia and Africa, whenever and wherever imperial interests required.[79]

But European styles of muscular bonding remained, in India, strictly confined to the ranks of the army. Traditional religious rituals, both Moslem and Hindu, gave considerable scope to muscular expressions of piety, as we saw in the previous chapter. Yet when Mohandas Gandhi (d. 1948) began to organize a secular mass movement for independence in the 1930s, the crowds he assembled practiced civil disobedience with considerable effect, marching, without saluting, or resorting to any other concerted muscular expression of their cause.

The Ottoman empire, like India, encountered European drill before calisthenics had been invented; but the Turks *refused to* take lessons in military matters from westerners, and (with minor exceptions) persisted in their refusal until 1826 despite a succession of defeats by Austrian and Russian armies. Instead of swallowing European drill whole, as the Russians did, the Turks responded to their early defeats with an outburst of reforming zeal that aimed at recovering lost greatness by a more faithful adherence to hallowed practices of the past. Between 1656 and 1683, Ottoman armies met with sufficient success to confirm the wisdom of this reactionary reform, and subsequent defeats took a long time to discredit it.

One reason was that three of the most fanatical groups in Ottoman society that resisted the idea of imitating unbelievers were themselves sustained by their own styles of muscular bonding. Thousands of students in *madrassas*, aspiring to official employment as judges, for example, intoned sacred texts and prayed together in unison during much of their waking hours. These young men, together with dervishes (whose muscular methods for inducing trance were discussed in the previous chapter), regularly led crowds of pious protesters through the streets of Istanbul, threatening anyone who dared to propose what they viewed as dangerous innovation, military or otherwise. Such crowds were reinforced by a third group, the Janissaries, who traditionally marched together on ceremonial occasions. Because they possessed handguns, the Janissaries were able to defend their privileges and successfully checked almost every effort at military reform, until the sultan, made desperate by military failures against rebellious Greeks, used a small detachment of new-fangled artillery to massacre them in 1826. With that obstacle removed, he then hastened to establish a new army on European models.

Drill soon shaped the new Turkish army into an effective force, but this success had the unexpected effect of creating a community seriously at odds with its environing civil society. By the early twentieth century many officers had become revolutionaries of one sort or another, and most ended up supporting an angry Turkish nationalism. The result, of course, was disruption of the empire and the emergence of a ruthlessly secular, modernizing republic after World War I.

Thus muscular bonding was influential both in supporting conservative reaction among the Ottomans, and also in sustaining a new style of army that soon became malignantly rebellious against the polyethnicity of traditional Ottoman society. All too obviously, paralyzing polarization delayed effective response to European pressures until it was too late for the Ottoman empire to survive. The Mughal empire did no better; and, in fact, stubborn tensions between traditions of Moslem piety and successful adaptation to western techniques and organization still persist in every Moslem country.[80]

In the Far East, responses to European pressures were almost equally disruptive, but reforms eventually became much more successful. Even more than in China, Japan's encounter with European military and political methods aroused fiercely contradictory responses. When St. Francis Xavier arrived on their shores in 1549, the Japanese interest in European guns and Christianity was far greater than anywhere else in Asia. In the next half century large numbers of arquebusiers, equipped with guns manufactured in Japan in imitation of European weapons, played decisive part in the warfare that led to Japan's unification in 1587 under an upstart warlord, Toyotomi Hideyoshi. Presumably, drill played its usual part in consolidating the rival armies of the age, but I have not found any discussion of how the Japanese trained their new gun-carrying infantry. In any case, this sudden development was reversed and undone after 1600, when a new supreme warlord, Tokugawa Ieyasu (d. 1616), established the Tokugawa shogunate. In the next half century the new rulers of Japan chose to patronize Confucianism, persecute Christians, and disarm commoners so as to safeguard themselves from rebellion at home and assure a monopoly of arms for the landowning class of samurai warriors. Manufacture of handguns ceased, and existing stocks were collected and destroyed.[81] Simultaneously, Japanese were prohibited from leaving the country, and legal contact with the outside world was limited to Nagasaki, where a single Dutch ship was permitted to conduct trade from an island in the harbor once a year.

Then, after two centuries of isolation, the balance swung back to energetic imitation of European and American military and civil institutions, beginning in 1867. An army and navy in the European style were set up in 1872. Universal military training for all young men met with such success that in 1894–95 the Japanese defeated China in war and began a career of imperial expansion in Korea that reached its spectacular apex half a century later in 1942. Civilian mobilization was just as energetic. Physical education was decreed for schools in 1872, followed by the introduction of military drill in 1886, Swedish gymnastics in 1913, and *judo* and *kindo* (traditional forms of dueling) in 1920.[82] Defeat in World War II did little to discourage gymnastic and other mass exercises in Japan; it is still customary in many Japanese factories to begin each day with calisthenics that express and confirm the group solidarity of the workforce. Moreover, as we saw earlier, a Buddhist association of laymen, the Soka Gakkai, elaborated rhythmic muscular ways of defining the group's collective identity in post-war Japan, and attained considerable political importance by launching its own political party.

Building on long-standing Buddhist traditions of muscular comradeship, it thus appears that the Japanese have successfully tapped the emotional solidarity aroused by keeping together in time both in military and civil contexts. It is, presumably, one of the secrets of their remarkable social cohesion and recent economic success.

China long tried to resist the West by paying as little attention as possible to what the "south sea barbarians" were up to. Smug inattention sufficed, until China's enormous success in extinguishing the nomad threat from the steppes began to wear out towards the end of the eighteenth century. By then, popula-

tion growth created hardship among the poor so that smouldering discontents, often associated with Buddhist and other heterodox sects, burst sporadically into flame, beginning in 1775.
The greatest such revolt, the Taiping Rebellion (1850–1864),
made the instability of Chinese society all too clear to imperial
authorities. Their difficulties were enormously enhanced by
their simultaneous embroilment with European intruders, who
had acquired new footholds in China after the Opium War of
1838–1841. By that time European guns outclassed Chinese
weapons, and the morale and training of China's armed establishments made them no match even for small European expeditionary forces.

Reform from the top to control rebellion from below, while
also holding Europeans at arm's length, presented China's
rulers with an insoluble dilemma. Borrowing European military methods might work against peasant rebellion, but it
required reformers to embrace the foreign ways they wished to
repulse. A few Chinese military leaders made the attempt
anyway; but they were no more successful than early Ottoman
military reformers had been, and for the same reason. Still,
drill and gymnastics did gain lasting foothold in China when
German military instructors brought them to Tientsin Military
Academy in 1885, even though these practices scarcely affected
most Chinese soldiers until after World War I.[83]

Simultaneously, Christian missionaries, who gained access
to China after 1858, introduced calisthenics through the
YMCA and mission schools without in the least intending to
link such muscular exercises with the expression of Chinese
national feeling, as actually happened after 1949.

Long before that, resistance to foreigners and affirmation of
Chinese identity did find their own form of muscular expression through the so-called Boxer Rebellion of 1898–1900. The
Fists of United Righteousness, to give them their proper name,
combined traditions of local self-defense and exercise in the
martial arts with Buddhist and Taoist traditions of stylized

exercises supposed to improve health and confer supernatural powers. The Boxers' exercises, as staged in public places in Chinese villages of Shantung province, were aimed at inducing a god to enter the body of each participant. When the god came, and a state of ecstasy had been attained, it was supposed that the divine visitor would confer invulnerability on the initiate.[84]

Such hopes proved vain when attacks on foreign missionaries (beginning in 1897), and hesitant support for the Boxers from the imperial court brought European and American soldiers to the scene. Defeat was sudden and complete. Chinese resistance to foreigners then took other paths, led first by Kuomintang Nationalists, then by Communists. Both these revolutionary parties opted for military modernization along European lines, and both resorted to European styles of drill and calisthenics as a way of developing the national spirit required to make China a great power once again.

When Chiang Kai-shek took over leadership of the Kuomintang in 1927, military drill almost entirely eclipsed official patronage of civilian expressions of muscular solidarity, although the Kuomintang continued to endorse physical education in schools. The Communists paid much more attention to civilian mobilization, and recognized the YMCA-style of calisthenics as an effective way of doing so. Thus it is not accidental that Chu Teh, commander of the Red Army, was a physical-training instructor before he became a soldier; and, while still a student, Mao Tse-tung published *A Study of Physical Culture* (1917) in which he declared that "the main practical consideration of physical culture is military heroism."[85] Accordingly, when they came to power in 1949, the Chinese Communists instituted daily nationwide broadcasts of calisthenic instruction, conducted in unison and to music. Presumably millions of Chinese responded and continue to respond obediently every morning. The hold that such exercises now have in China has become familiar to the rest of the world through TV broadcasts of thousands of school children, and of troops as well, moving in precise unison on Tiananmen Square.

Thus it appears that, like the Japanese, Chinese Communists brought into the open a long-standing tradition of muscular rituals, that had been practiced surreptitiously by heterodox sects, and began to link muscular movements in unison with active commitment to official policy. Assuredly, Mao Tse-tung and his followers met with far greater success than the imperial government did by toying with the Boxers.

But Chinese Communists probably also owed something to a revolutionary socialist tradition of muscular solidarity that began to assume distinctive forms when, in 1889, the International Socialist Congress proclaimed May Day to be a holiday for workingmen of all the world. In Austria, the Marxist politician Victor Adler (d. 1918) was particularly inventive in modeling socialist May Day parades on Vienna's Corpus Christi celebrations.[86] Others elsewhere soon followed suit. I have no knowledge of how the clenched fist salute and other muscular manifestations of Marxist revolutionary identity came into use, but such outward manifestations of collective consciousness flourished among Marxist parties as long as they remained in opposition to established governments. When Marxists seized power in Russia in 1917, however, the burdens of office together with accompanying repression of dissenters quickly eroded party spirit, and, under Stalin, May Day parades and other public demonstrations of support for the regime became more and more completely militarized.

As Stalin's revolutionary impulse flagged, Mao Tse-tung in China and Hitler in Germany intensified their efforts to mobilize civil society. I only surmise that Mao's emphasis on muscular expression of political commitment was influenced by European socialist precedents; but for Hitler there is no doubt, since he tells us explicitly how profoundly he was stirred by Vienna's May Day parades in his youth. In his own words: "For nearly two hours I stood there watching with bated breath the gigantic human dragon slowly winding by." He was both attracted by how the "dragon" transcended the everyday human scale, and simultaneously appalled by the sight of "masses of those no longer belonging to the people."[87]

As we all know, in due course he set out to remedy their alienation by organizing marches and other muscular manifestations of a new German national-socialist identity. In the struggle for power, party uniforms (an innovation of Mussolini's Fascists, modeled perhaps on Garibaldi's Red Shirts) distinguished the marching SA and SS units from foes and uncommitted civilians alike. Then, after the Nazis took office, the Hitler stiff-arm salute and the Heil Hitler greeting decreed in 1934 required everyone to give overt muscular expression of loyalty to the regime at frequent intervals every day. Party festivals and public rituals, scattered throughout the year in obvious competiton with Christian holidays, gave further occasion for muscular and verbal expression of commitment to the regime. Of these, the annual rallies at Nuremberg became the largest and most spectacular.[88]

Hitler's belief that shared blood was the only community that mattered prepared him to take seriously the muscular, subverbal level of human interaction. Blood, after all, manifested itself more in actions and feeling than in words and reasoning. Accordingly, his public appearances were quite consciously aimed at arousing emotions, and he remained on the lookout for ways to enhance the emotional level of communication with his followers. He is once reputed to have said: "The concluding meeting at Nuremberg must be exactly as solemnly and ceremonially performed as a service of the Catholic Church." And Albert Speer won Hitler's confidence in part by creating a "cathedral of light" for those rallies by pointing searchlights into the sky.[89] But American football rituals also came to Hitler's attention when a Harvard graduate, "Putzi" Hanfstaengl, played the "Fight Song" in his company and explained how American undergraduates were wont to behave on Saturday afternoons. "That is it. That is what we need for the movement," Hitler is reported to have exclaimed.[90]

These and other scraps of information make it clear that Hitler was conscious and deliberate in exploiting Germans' emotional responses to keeping together in time in order to create national solidarity on a thoroughly subrational level. "The audience is not being informed," he once remarked, when asked about his rhetorical techniques, "it is made to perform; and its performance makes history."[91]

Hitler was, sadly but surely, right in making that claim. His hearers did make history, and he captivated the German people so profoundly that nearly all of them remained loyal to him throughout World War II and obedient until the bitter end. Hitler's words and ideas were little more than a scum riding on top of the visceral bonding that Nazi political techniques created, very largely by means of movement in unison and other muscular manifestations of shared "blood." Other factors of course played a part: resentment against the Versailles treaty, long-standing anti-Semitism, economic depression. But without the emotional residues created by the multiple muscular expressions of Nazi *Gleichshaltung,* I very much doubt whether the National Socialist German Workers' Party could have fastened its hold on the German people as strongly as it did. Hitler's career, in fact, offers a dark and ominous proof of how keeping together in time can unite and barbarize a whole nation, regardless of how well educated, highly skilled and sophisticated it may be.

SINCE WORLD WAR II, widespread revulsion against everything associated with the Nazis has discredited mass muscular manifestations of political attachments. But what is ushered from the front door creeps in at the back, as illustrated by the rhythmic movements of sports fans at football games, and by the continued effervescence of innumerable religious groups in all parts of the earth.

Euphoric response to keeping together in time is too deeply implanted in our genes to be exorcized for long. It remains the most powerful way to create and sustain a community that we have at our command. And since we are social creatures, we need communities to guide our lives and give them meaning. In big, anonymous cities, the need is acute. It follows that in an age when more and more persons find themselves adrift in such cities, muscular bonding is likely to become more rather than less important in defining and redefining who we are and with whom we share a common identity.

This is nothing new, as this book has tried to show; and as long as human beings survive on the face of the earth, keeping together in time will surely continue to make history, as it has throughout the past.

# Conclusion

SINCE WORLD WAR II, repugnance against Hitlerism has discredited rhythmic muscular expressions of political and other sorts of ideological attachment throughout the western world. Distrust of visceral responses to such exercises prevails. Youths, especially of the middle class, cling strenuously to their individuality, while even the most politically innocuous expressions of muscular bonding (for example, folk dancing, marching bands, and choral societies) struggle to survive in a time when watching TV in the privacy of the home has become the predominant form of mass entertainment. Religious sects that give scope to muscular bonding through song and dance fare somewhat better in competition with TV, but in Europe and the United States they affect only a few. Africa and Latin America are where enthusiastic, muscularly uninhibited religion flourishes best. Among the pious of the western world, TV evangelism and decorous congregational worship, restrained by pews, is what prevails. Sports fans do express team loyalty by resorting to cheers and rhythmic muscular movements in the stands. Sport, indeed, is what the American public seems to care about most; and the situation is not very different in western European lands.

In China, Korea, and Japan, however, calisthenics and other forms of mass movement in unison continue to flourish with the uninhibited support of political and economic leaders, despite (or even because of) past associations with Japan's imperial ambitions. Schools, factories, political parties, and, in Japan, religious sects all rely on rhythmic movement in unison to establish and confirm collective solidarity among those who participate. Confucian family discipline and a traditional reliance on formal education as a practical path to personal and family advancement do much to explain the striking economic growth of these countries since World War II. But in all probability muscular bonding also contributes to their success, by creating and enhancing social cohesion and willing cooperation at all levels of society.

Since muscular bonding through dance and song was an important cement for human communities in times past, our contemporary neglect of these forms of sociality appears to be aberrant from the human norm. Perhaps, indeed, it will not long endure. Human beings desperately need to belong to communities that give guidance and meaning to their lives; and moving rhythmically while giving voice together is the surest, most speedy, and efficacious way of creating and sustaining such communities that our species has ever hit upon. Words and ideals matter and are always invoked; but keeping together in time arouses warm emotions of collective solidarity and erases personal frustrations as words, by themselves, cannot do. Large and complex human societies, in all probability, cannot long maintain themselves without such kinesthetic undergirding. Ideas and ideals are not enough. Feelings matter too, and feelings are inseparable from their gestural and muscular expression.

The future is of course opaque, but it seems obvious that human society is moving away from a long-standing duality between urban and rural patterns of life. When cities first arose, the gap between rural and urban modes of life was enormous. Cities were parasites, requiring a continual flow of food and of migrants from the countryside to sustain themselves. One result of this relationship was that biological and cultural continuity depended on what happened in villages—and in Eurasia, also on what tribes of steppe nomads did. Cities were biological sink holes that had to be continually replenished from the surrounding countryside. That ceased to be true when modern public health measures checked lethal infectious disease, starting a little more than a century ago; but acute strains on the nurture of the young in contemporary cities all round the world suggests that human beings have not yet managed to work out an enduring, biologically and culturally self-sufficient style of urban living.

In villages, children learned the arts of life without conscious design simply by living and working with their elders, since workplace and domicile were the same. In cities, after the industrial revolution, workplace and domicile separated, so that adults disappeared from their children's view for many hours a day. The nurture of the young and transmission of culture from generation to generation therefore ceased to be automatic. Schools and other institutions took over part of the job, but an essential factor in stabilizing industrialized urban society was a continued, massive influx of newcomers who had been nurtured to adulthood in the age-old way by day-long association with their parents in the countryside.

This precarious balance now threatens to collapse, since village patterns of nurture are coming under unparalleled pressure from urban-based radio and TV broadcasting, reinforced by rapidly expanding commercialization of what used to be subsistence peasant farming. As a result, urban society, as it reaches out to embrace the rural majority of humankind, runs an increasing risk of irremediable unraveling because of breakdowns in the nurture of the young.[1]

In times past, village-wide dancing on festival occasions relieved personal discontents and bound rural society together far more effectively than anything that words, ideas, or ideals could do. It is plausible to suppose that community dancing was essential to the on-going stability of village life, upon which cities and all the works of civilization ultimately depended. But if, as seems to be happening, villagers' accustomed style of life dissolves away, merging into an urban-based global economy and commercialized cosmopolitan society, long-term viability will demand far-ranging adjustments of human behavior in which keeping together in time is sure to play an important part.

The dilemma is acute. On the one hand, human beings need the support and guidance in their everyday living that has always been provided by membership in small face-to-face communities where neighbors know one another personally. On the other hand, such communities have to learn to get along more or less peacefully with strangers. Ever since civilizations first arose, the human majority, living on the land, accommodated itself to powerful outsiders who demanded rents and taxes from them. Such intrusions, however, did not prevent village communities from maintaining their own integrity and cultural traditions, despite subordination to distant masters. But in our time the invasion of urban ideas and ideals is far more powerful than ever before, thanks to the Pied Piper of TV broadcasting, reinforced by the fact that in many rural landscapes there is not enough land available for young people to continue to live and work as their parents do, even if they wished to.

The ancient response to anomie and the dissolution of face-to-face communities in urban commercial contexts was the invention of portable congregational religions. The vigor of similar religious groups in Third World cities today shows that this response has lost none of its efficacy. Perhaps, indeed, muscularly vivacious sects and more subdued, ritualized religious assemblies will turn out to be the principal human response to the difficulties of living well in our global flow-through economy. On the other hand, new, inventive, and hitherto unexplored modes of creating and sustaining local communities within the context of worldwide urbanity must not be ruled out.

Whatever happens, our capacity for muscular bonding will not disappear. If wisely aroused, it could help to create and sustain new sorts of communities that might turn out to be thoroughly compatible with the global economic exchanges upon which we have come to depend. Dance groups, choral societies, athletic associations, and the like do not need to be harnessed to rival nationalisms or other confrontational identities. The shared euphoria aroused by keeping together in time is intrinsically diffuse, without definite external object or significance. Ideas and words can therefore turn the warm sentiments of group solidarity it arouses in many different directions. Hitler's brutal, suicidal path is not the only way to go, nor does the enormous variety of existing religious groups exhaust possible meanings assignable to this human capability. Benign, humane, and secular ideals can also be nourished by muscular bonding within human groups, large and small.

In the long range, such expressions of the most primitive form of human communication are likely to multiply, since benign, humane, and secular ideals are especially well fitted to sustain the efficiency of the global exchange system we are struggling to adapt to. Global exchanges maximize human wealth and power, and most people, most of the time, prefer wealth and power to their opposites, however much they may quarrel over its distribution.

The resulting quarrels bulk large in everyday consciousness, but that should not blind us to the fact that in the long run institutional arrangements that increase total productivity and permit better satisfaction of human wants do tend to prevail. It follows that what we need in our time is to impart greater attractive force to human groups that facilitate global exchanges by decrying violence and minimizing confrontations with neighbors. Muscular expressions of membership in such communities, by consolidating them and enhancing their emotional vibrancy, can conceivably take the place that village dancing did in times past by providing a fundamental cement for all levels of human society once again.

WHETHER OR NOT such a future lies ahead, it is still worth while to become aware of the muscular, rhythmic dimension of human sociality. It is and always has been a powerful force at work among humankind, whether for good or ill. Successive levels of communication—muscular and gestural, then vocal and verbal, then written and mathematical—are what made *Homo sapiens* the dominant species it has become. Our future, like our past, depends on how we utilize these modes of coordinating common effort for agreed purposes. So far, the human record is one of extraordinary success in wringing more and more food and other forms of energy out of the natural environment. There is no reason to suppose that possibilities of increasing our power over natural flows of matter and energy have been exhausted, or that human inventiveness has ceased to operate. On the contrary, inventiveness can be counted on to exploit sentiments aroused by keeping together in time in the future as in the past. This primitive level of sociality has lost none of its power to create communities, and since we need communities as acutely as ever, opportunities for invention that will help to shape social solidarity in the future are unusually wide open.

Realizing that this is the case may even help to guide invention along benign and sustainable paths. But whether or not we are conscious of the different communicative levels that interact to define each different group we belong to, the historic process of choosing between competing identities and loyalties will continue indefinitely into the future, affecting every human life. This is and always has been the principal moral problem humans confront. To what, and with whom do we belong? Dance, drill, and other rhythmic muscular exercises have always played a part in answering these questions.

They will continue to do so as long as the gestural, muscular level of communication continues to bind human beings together into emotionally vibrant groups that give meaning and purpose to human experience.

Our contemporary disregard of this aspect of human sociality is unwise and probably also unsustainable over the long haul. Time will tell. In the meanwhile it is something to mull over, wonder about, and—for bolder spirits—to experiment with.

# Notes

## 1. Muscular Bonding

1. John H. Faris, "The Impact of Basic Combat Training: The Role of the Drill Sergeant," in Nancy Goldman and David R. Segal, eds., *The Social Psychology of Military Service*, vol. 6 of Sage Research Progress Series on War, Revolution and Peacekeeping (Newbury Park, Calif., 1976), p. 13, has this to say: "Strong feelings of affection for their drill sergeants are very common in trainees. In a sample of 107 trainees interviewed over a one and a half year period, 91% responded to the question: 'What do you think of your drill sergeant?' in a positive way. None were unqualifiedly negative." Faris was surprised by this response, but came up with banal and (to me) entirely unconvincing explanations.

2. A peevish reader of the manuscript of this book, after declaring that he had hated army drill, mocked this phrase, saying it could only apply to muscle-builders showing off on California beaches. I retain it nonetheless as the most economical way to refer to a real aspect of human behavior, even though isolated individuals can indeed consciously repress the euphoric affect of keeping together in time when compelled to take part in something they dislike or fear or hate.

3. William H. McNeill, *The Pursuit of Power* (Chicago, 1982), pp. 125–133.

4. But as one expert remarked almost twenty years ago: "To the author's knowledge no laboratory research has directly examined ritual trance incorporating kinetic movement such as dancing." Barbara W. Lex, "Physiological Aspects of Ritual Trance," *Journal of Altered States of Consciousness*, 2 (1975) 118. As far as I can discover this still remains the case.

5. Raymond Prince, "The Endorphins," *Ethos,* 10 (1982) 311 and *passim;* Wolfgang G. Jilek, "Altered States of Consciousness in North American Indian Ceremonials," *Ethos,* 10 (1982) 326–343. This entire issue was devoted to endorphins and their putative role in trance and other altered states of consciousness, but the authors rely mainly on speculation in the absence of definite experimental results.

6. Robert Plutchik and Henry Kellerman, eds., *Emotion: Theory, Research and Experience,* 5 vols. (New York, 1980–1989), III, 128–132.

7. Perhaps, as one popularizing writer says, "Emotional information fed to the brain enters via a different neural network. . . . New research shows that the emotions have a separate system of nerve pathways through the limbic system to the cortex, allowing emotional signals to avoid conscious control." Robert Ornstein, *The Evolution of Consciousness* (New York, 1991), p. 80. Unfortunately he does not footnote this assertion.

8. I consulted Francis Lenkel, *Introduction to Physiological Psychology,* 3rd ed. (St. Louis, 1976); Robert Plutchik, *Emotion: A Psychoevolutionary Synthesis* (New York, 1980); Ernst Gellhorn, *Principles of Autonomic-Somatic Integration* (Minneapolis, 1967) for light on the physiology of emotions, without finding more than opaque elaboration of ideas advanced by Walter Cannon in 1915 about the roles of the sympathetic nervous system and the hypothalamus in controlling the exhibition of emotion.

9. That does not prevent scholars from writing about it. See Eugene G. d'Aquili et al., *The Spectrum of Ritual,* (New York, 1979), pp. 157–158. He declares that the simultaneous discharge "of both autonomic systems creates a state of stimulation in the forebrain bundle, generating not only a pleasurable sensation, but, under proper conditions, a sense of oneness with conspecifics." Although as far as I can tell d'Aquili lacks experimental basis for such assertions, they conform quite exactly to my recollections of how drill affected me.

10. Both Andrew Neher, "A Physiological Explanation of Unusual Behavior in Ceremonies Involving Drums," *Human Biology,* 34 (1962) 151–160 and William Walter Sargant, *Battle for the Mind: A Physiology of Conversion and Brainwashing* (New York, 1957), p. 106, attribute trance or convulsive behavior that is sometimes excited by dancing to enhanced or altered brain waves in the cortex; similarly, V. J. Walter and W. Gray Walter, "The Central Effects of Rhythmic Sensory Stimulation," *EEG and Chemical Neurophysiology,* 1 (1949) 57–86 sought to

detect differences between normal and epileptic persons' responses to rhythmic sensory stimuli but got no meaningful results. Experiments directed towards extreme states have not produced cures nor really traced the paths of connection between altered brain waves and overt behavior or emotional state. The less intense, far commoner, and historically more important warm emotional response to rhythmic movement experienced in the company of others seems never to have attracted scientific attention.

11. Loring M. Danforth, "The Role of Dance in the Ritual Therapy of the Anastenasia," *Modern Greek Studies,* 5 (1979) 159.

12. Richard Katz, "Accepting 'Boiling Energy': The Experience of !Kia Healing among the !Kung," *Ethos,* 19 (1982) 348.

13. A. R. Radcliffe-Brown, *The Andaman Islanders* (Cambridge, 1922), pp. 252–253.

14. Judith L. Hanna, "African Dance and the Warrior Tradition," *Journal of Asian and African Studies,* 12 (1977) 119.

15. Hilda Kuper, *An African Aristocracy: Rank among the Swazi of Bechuanaland* (Oxford, 1947), p. 224.

16. Felicitas D. Goodman, *Speaking in Tongues* (Chicago, 1972), pp. 76–79, makes this suggestion.

17. Maurice de Saxe, *Reveries on the Art of War,* trans. Thomas R. Phillips (Harrisburg, Pa., 1944), pp. 30–31.

18. Personal letter to W. H. McNeill, March 1991.

19. Edward A. Shils and Morris Janowitz, "Cohesion and Disintegration in the Wehrmacht in World War II," *Public Opinion Quarterly,* 12 (1948) 280–315.

20. Jesse Glen Gray, *The Warriors: Reflections on Men in Battle* (New York, 1973), pp 52–55.

21. This is not a new idea. Cf. Havelock Ellis, *The Dance of Life,* (Boston, 1923), p. 63: "The participants in a dance, as all observers of savages have noted, exhibit a wonderful unison; they are, as it were, fused into a single being, stirred by a single impulse. Social unification is thus accomplished. Apart from war, this is the chief factor making for social solidarity in primitive life; it was indeed the best training for war."

# 2. Human Evolution

1. Wolfgang Kohler, *The Mentality of Apes,* trans. Ella Winter, 2nd ed. (New York, 1976).

2. Cf. Frans de Waal, *Chimpanzee Politics: Power and Sex among the Apes* (New York, 1982).

3. The dilemma is not fundamentally different from what anthropologists face in studying simple human communities. The mere arrival of a mysterious stranger in the person of the anthropologist changes the situation in ways beyond exact measurement. Similarly, chimpanzee behavior surely altered when Goodall started to set out bananas at special feeding stations and began to approach them in the open with notebook in hand. Still, careful observation has since shown that bands learn new ways of behaving from time to time anyway, so that the shock of close encounter with humans may not differ altogether from other encounters that take place in their world, and certainly does not erase deep-seated patterns of social interaction among the individual animals concerned.

4. Geza Teleki, *The Predatory Behavior of Wild Chimpanzees* (Lewisburg, Pa., 1973), pp. 34–37. Goodall's popular accounts are misleading, inasmuch as she leaves the impression that she was observing truly wild behavior.

5. Jane Goodall, *My Friends, the Wild Chimpanzees* (Washington, D.C., 1967), p. 77. This volume supplements the text with very instructive photographs of such a rain dance.

6. Adolph Schultz, *The Life of Primates* (New York, 1967), p. 223. Barbara Smuts once observed four chimpanzees engage in simultaneous display behavior after returning from a raid into another band's territory. Their celebratory relief of tension lasted for several minutes, and involved closely synchronized extreme exertion—swinging on vines across a stream and the like. Personal communication, June 1994.

7. Vernon Reynolds and Frances Reynolds, "Chimpanzees of the Budongo Forest," in Irven DeVore, ed., *Primate Behavior* (New York, 1965), p. 369.

8. Kohler, *The Mentality of Apes*, pp. 314–315.

9. Tetsuro Matsuzawa, "Colour Naming and Classification in Chimpanzees," *Journal of Human Evolution*, 14 (1985) 283–291 shows that human and chimp color recognition are identical, even for intermediate tints. See other quite amazing instances, for example, of how a chimpanzee once drove a car in Los Angeles traffic, recounted by Geoffrey H. Bourne, *The Ape People* (New York, 1971), p. 156 and *passim*.

A band of chimpanzees living at large has also been known to imitate humans, learning how to hammer palm oil nuts with stones to extract the nourishing kernel, which they cannot get otherwise. Adrian Kort-landt, "The Use of Stone Tools by Wild-Living Chimpanzees and Earliest Hominids," *Journal of Human Evolution,* 15 (1986) 72–132.

10. E. C. Holmes et al., "Stochastic Models of Molecular Evolution and the Estimation of Phylogeny and Rates of Nucleotide Substitution in the Hominid Primates," *Journal of Human Evolution,* 18 (1989) 775–794 gives 7.5 millions years ago as a probable date, but according to Richard Wrangham, "chimp-human divergence is more often viewed at c. 6 million years now." Personal communication, November 1994.

11. Jane Goodall was surprised, for such behavior contradicted ten years' observation of peaceable interaction among all members of the band. See Jane Goodall, "Highlights of Current Research," in Paul G. Heltrie and Linda Marquardt, eds., *Understanding Chimpanzees* (Cambridge, Mass., 1989), pp. 2–21, and Jane Goodall, *The Chimpanzees of Gombe: Patterns of Behavior* (Cambridge, Mass., 1986), pp. 488–534.

12. Anne Pusey, "Intercommunity Transfer of Chimpanzees in Gombe National Park," in David A. Hamburg and Elizabeth R. McCown, eds., *The Great Apes* (Menlo Park, Calif., 1979), pp. 465–480. This of course assured the sort of gene circulation that any population must have to maintain genetic variety and flexibility. See also Jean Pierre Bocquet-Appel, "Small Populations, Demography and Paleoanthropological Inferences," *Journal of Human Evolution,* 14 (1985) 683–91.

13. Richard W. Wrangham, "Sex Differences in Chimpanzee Dispersion," in Hamburg and McCown, eds, *The Great Apes,* pp. 481–488; Joseph H. Manson and Richard W. Wrangham, "Intergroup Aggression in Chimpanzees and Humans," *Current Anthropology,* 32 (1991) 369–392; Michael P. Ghiglieri, "Sociobiology of the Great Apes and the Hominid Ancestor," *Journal of Human Evolution,* 16 (1987) 319–357.

14. Frans de Waal, "Food Sharing and Reciprocal Obligations among Chimpanzees," *Journal of Human Evolution,* 18 (1989) 433–459; Frans de Waal, "Sex Differences in the Formation of Coalitions among Chimpanzees," *Ethology and Biology,* 5 (1984) 239–255.

15. De Waal, *Chimpanzee Politics: Power and Sex among the Apes,* and Frans de Waal, *Peacemaking among Primates* (Cambridge, Mass., 1989) describe in exquisite detail how alliances were arranged and fell apart among chimpanzees in the Arnhem zoo.

16. It is interesting to reflect on how even semi-bipedal posture may have affected male chimpanzee agonistic behavior. Since fighting in-

volved first seizing hold of the enemy with hands and then biting his flesh, numbers do indeed become decisive. Three males attacking a far stronger foe could still expect to prevail, as long as two of them seized an arm apiece, and held tight while the third attacked the immobilized enemy's throat, genitals, and other vulnerable parts.

17. Barbara Smuts informed me (June 1994) that Richard Wrangham had encountered a much larger band of chimpanzees in Uganda, comprising up to 45 males. But his observations remain unpublished and he himself was unavailable when I sought to communicate with him.

18. A superior food base for the band that remained close to the feeding station may also have helped it to prevail against its rivals.

19. Yishisada Nishida and Mariko Hiraiko-Hasegawa, "Chimpanzees and Bonobos: Cooperative Relationships among Males," in Barbara Smuts et al., eds., *Primate Societies* (Chicago, 1987), pp. 165–177.

20. Chimpanzees are sexually promiscuous, and the alpha male does not seem to have any special access to estrus females. Young males are at least partially excluded from sexual intercourse, however, hovering around the margins of the group as a rule.

21. Ghiglieri, "Sociobiology of the Great Apes and the Hominid Ancestor," 335; Richard W. Wrangham, "Evolution of Social Structure," in Smuts et al., eds., *Primate Societies,* pp. 282–296.

22. My ancestors in the Scottish Hebrides behaved in this way as recently as 1745, treating anyone who was not kin as foe.

23. See Chapter One. I am tempted to speculate further that bipedality, freeing hands to hold sticks, may have been important in allowing the first dancers to keep together in time, since establishing a regular muscular rhythm is enormously facilitated by listening to the tap of a drum—even if, at first, there was only a stick hitting the ground at regular intervals.

24. I rely on two fine textbooks for this summary: Roger Lewin, *Human Evolution: An Illustrated Introduction,* 3rd ed. (Boston, 1993); and Richard G. Klein, *The Human Career* (Chicago, 1989). It is worth pointing out that many gaps and uncertainties exist. Substantial remains (such as intact crania or complete jaw bones) of *Homo erectus* are only known from Asia, where they were once referred to as Peking and Java man. The bones from Africa that have been assigned to the same species are too fragmentary to make the classification definite. Parallel uncertainty surrounds the origin of *Homo sapiens* because of similarly fragmentary skeletal discoveries.

25. Dorothy L. Cheyney and Robert M. Seyforth, *How Monkeys See the World* (Chicago, 1990), pp. 127–243 and *passim*; Gordon W. Hewes, "Primate Communication and the Gestural Origin of Language," *Current Anthropology*, 14 (1973) 5–24; Roger S. Fouts, "Capacities for Language in Great Apes," in Russell H. Tuttle, ed., *Socioecology and Psychology of Primates* (The Hague, 1975), pp. 371–390.

26. Thomas K. Pitcairn and Irenaus Eibl-Eibesfeldt, "Concerning the Evolution of Nonverbal Communication in Man," in Martin E. Hahn and Edward C. Simmel, eds., *Communicative Behavior and Evolution* (New York, 1976), pp. 81–113; Ray L. Birdwhistell, *Kinesics and Context: Essays in Body Motion Communication* (Philadelphia, 1970).

27. I rely largely on Derek Bickerton, *Language and Species* (Chicago, 1981) for these remarks about pidgin and articulated speech.

28. Bickerton (p. 138) expressly connects *Homo erectus* with the emergence of pidgin, but I have discovered no discussion of dancing as part of human evolution. This suggestion thus rests entirely on my own intuition—and personal experience of drill.

29. The idea that larger communities affected evolution when our ancestors started living on the African savanna does appear in learned discussion, but without connecting the change to the emotional impact of dancing as in the ponderous prose of James Steele, "Hominid Evolution and Primate Social Cognition," *Journal of Human Evolution*, 18 (1989) 421: "Increased social competition resulting from larger grouping patterns, the latter a response to predation risks, is hypothesized to have presented the dominant selection pressure for human cognitive and socially manipulative skills, and thus for hominid brain and language evolution." See also Lars Rodseth, et al., "The Human Community as a Primate Society," *Current Anthropology*, 32 (June 1991) 240: "Collective rituals temporarily create a stable, face-to-face society—a kind of 'human troop'—from the routine fragmentation and solitude of the human community. At moments of communitas, interindividual differences are effaced, multiple levels of social organization dissolved, family, clan and other allegiances temporarily forgotten, leaving a seamless social whole." The authors do not specifically mention dance, but they were writing about Australian corroborees and similar ceremonies where dancing is indeed central.

30. Glynn Isaac, "The Food Sharing Behavior of Proto-Human Hominids," *Scientific American*, 238 (April, 1978) 90–108.

31. Kim Hill, "Hunting in Human Evolution," *Journal of Human Evolution*, 11 (1982) 524.

32. The phrase comes from William McGrew and Anna T. C. Feistner, "Two Primate Models for the Evolution of Human Food Sharing: Chimpanzees and Callitrichids," in Jerome Barkow et al., eds., *The Adapted Mind* (New York, 1992), p. 232. See Jane Goodall Von Lawick, *In the Shadow of Man* (New York, 1971), p. 205: "Often we have seen chimpanzees actually break off portions of their meat and hand them to begging individuals"; see also her more academic account of chimpanzee hunting and meat eating, Jane Goodall, *The Chimpanzees of Gombe: Patterns of Behavior* (Cambridge, Mass., 1986), pp. 267–312. On chimpanzee hunting see also Teleki, *The Predatory Behavior of Wild Chimpanzees*, and Geza Teleki, "The Omnivorous Diet and Eclectic Feeding Habits of Chimpanzees in Gombe National Park, Tanzania," in Robert S. Harding and Geza Teleki, eds., *Omnivorous Primates: Gathering and Hunting in Human Evolution* (New York, 1981), pp. 303–343.

33. Other bands hunt lizards, a prey which is neglected at Gombe, suggesting that hunting behavior is at least partially learned. Teleki, "The Omnivorous Diet and Eclectic Feeding Habits of Chimpanzees in Gombe National Park, Tanzania," in Harding and Teleki, *Omnivorous Primates*, p. 325.

34. Teleki, *The Predatory Behavior of Wild Chimpanzees*, p. 53.

35. Only horses and camels sweat all over the body as we do; and it is no accident that these two beasts eventually came to play such a prominent role in transport and communication. See David R. Carrier, "The Energetic Paradox of Human Running and Hominid Evolution," *Current Anthropology*, 25 (1984) p. 484.

36. P. E. Wheeler, "The Evolution of Bi-Pedality and Loss of Functional Body Hair in Hominids," *Journal of Human Evolution*, 13 (1984) 90–98; Carrier, "The Energetic Paradox," 483–491.

37. George B. Schaller and Gordon R. Lowther, "The Relevance of Carnivore Behavior to the Study of Early Hominids," *Southwest Journal of Anthropology*, 25 (1969) 329.

38. Eagles and hawks are also daytime hunters, but scarcely competed with humans for prey. Yet here, too, it is interesting to observe that some hawks have been tamed and even induced to share their prey with humans.

39. Chimpanzees are diurnal and, like humans, rely on eyesight more than nocturnal animals do. The primacy of sight among our senses

therefore probably antedates savanna existence, but daytime hunting and gathering in open landscapes surely put an extra premium on keen eyesight, visual memory, and enlargement of the visual processing capacity of the brain.

40. The extreme position is represented by Lewis R. Binford, "Were There Elephant Hunters at Torralba?" in Mathew H. Nitecki and Doris V. Nitecki, eds., *The Evolution of Human Hunting* (New York, 1988), p. 47. Binford stated flatly that hominids were not successful as hunters as late as 200,000 years ago and that firm evidence for hunting big game only begins with modern men of the Upper Paleolithic, that is, some 25,000 years ago. This discussion was triggered by the discovery that modern !Kung hunters and gatherers in the Kalahari desert derive only a small part of their caloric intake from hunting. See Richard B. Lee and Irven De Vore, eds., *Man the Hunter* (Chicago, 1968). But what can be captured and killed in a marginal habitat like the Kalahari is not a good model for human exploitation of the richer fauna of better watered regions.

41. McGrew and Feistner, "Two Primate Models for the Evolution of Human Food Sharing," in Barkow et al., eds., *The Adapted Mind*, p. 240; Kim Hill, "Hunting in Human Evolution," *Journal of Human Evolution*, 11 (1892) 521–44. For a judicious review of the argument over hunting and scavenging in human evolution see Robert Foley, *Hominid Evolution and Community Ecology: Prehistoric Human Adaptation in Biological Perspective* (London, 1984).

42. Herve Bochereus, "Isotopic Bio-Geochemistry of Fossil Vertebrate Collagen . . ." *Journal of Human Evolution*, 20 (1991) 481–492.

43. Reizo Harako, "The Cultural Ecology of Hunting Behavior among Mbuti Pygmies in the Iturbi Forest, Zaire," in Harding and Teleki, eds., *Omnivorous Primates*, p. 538.

44. Pat Shipman and Alan Walker, "The Costs of Becoming a Predator," *Journal of Human Evolution*, 18 (1989) 373–392.

45. Frans de Waal devised ingenious experiments at the Arnhem zoo whereby he gave special tidbits of vegetable food to different chimpanzees and watched how they repulsed some individuals and allowed others to share their treats. He concluded that memory of past kindnesses and clashes governed how the food was distributed. De Waal, "Food Sharing and Reciprocal Obligations among Chimpanzees," pp. 433–459.

46. Donald Symons, *The Evolution of Human Sexuality* (New York, 1979); L. L. Allen et al., "Demography and Human Origins," *American*

*Anthropologist,* 34 (1982) 888–896; McGrew and Feistner, "Two Primate Models for the Evolution of Human Food Sharing," in Barkow, ed., *The Adapted Mind,* pp. 229–248.

47. Herbivorous chimpanzees spend most of their waking hours gathering food, each animal feeding itself from what it finds in the forest, whereas lions spend as much as twenty hours a day lounging in the shade or sleeping.

48. Bone structures can often reveal the approximate age at death. On the assumption that skeletal changes proceeded in times past more or less as today, there seems good evidence that human life lengthened, and, in particular, females began to live past their child bearing age. Hill, "Hunting in Human Evolution," p. 541.

49. John L. Bradshaw, "The Evolution of Human Lateral Asymmetries: New Evidence and Second Thoughts," *Journal of Human Evolution,* 17 (1988) 633 makes this suggestion.

50. Published in Chicago, 1963.

# 3. Small Communities

1. Anthropologists have often asserted that dancing strengthens social bonds. Here is what one of the more literate and imaginative of them, A. R. Radcliffe-Brown, *The Andaman Islanders* (Cambridge, 1922), p. 252, has to say: "The precise sentiments varied with context, as when two groups danced together after a long period of separation and generated a feeling of harmony, when warriors danced to induce a collective anger before setting out to fight, or at a ceremony of peacemaking and reconciliation. On each occasion, the sentiments of unity and concord were intensely felt by every dancer, and this was the primary function of the dance."

2. Curt Sachs, *World History of the Dance* (New York, 1937); Alan Lomax, "Dance Style and Culture," in Alan Lomax et al., *Folk Song Style and Culture* (Washington D.C., 1968), pp. 223 ff.; Judith Lynn Hanna, *To Dance Is Human: A Theory of Non-verbal Communication* (Austin, 1979); and Walter Sorell, *Dance in Its Time* (New York, 1981) are examples of this effort. In Europe, folklorists have been ingenious and not entirely convincing in their efforts to reconstruct popular behavior. I did not delve into this literature, only consulting two samples of it: Maurice Alexis-Louis Louis, *Le folklore et la danse* (Paris, 1958) and Frances Rust, *Dance and Society* (London, 1969).

3. See Judith L. Hanna, "African Dance and the Warrior Tradition," *Journal of African Studies,* 12 (1977) 110–133.

4. Others have made comparable suggestions. For example, John Blacking, *The Anthropology of the Body* (London and New York, 1977), p. 225, says that dance "is a result of processes that have selective advantage," but he was thinking primarily or exclusively of dance as a way of practicing hunting and other practical skills.

5. Louis, *Le folklore et la danse.* Figure 2 reproduces this painting but gives no date.

6. Reproduced in Richard G. Kraus and Sarah A. Chapman, *History of the Dance in Art and Education,* 2nd ed. (Englewood Cliffs, N.J., 1981).

7. This was borne in upon me once when I greeted an esteemed colleague after a year's absence. I did not know that he was in the early stages of Parkinson's disease, but when we met his face remained frozen, and I felt as if he did not recognize me. Our brief talk therefore turned into an uncanny, disturbing encounter, at least on my part, for his facial immobility belied the warmth of greeting that his words purported to convey. But even though gestures certainly do carry a heavy emotive freight, efforts to decipher and give specific meaning to specific muscular movements have not gotten very far. See Ray L. Birdwhistell, *Kinesics and Context: Essays on Body Motion Communication* (Philadelphia, 1970); Martin E. Hahn and Edward C. Simmel, *Communicative Behavior and Evolution* (New York, 1976); and David McNeill, *Hand and Mind: What Gestures Reveal about Thought* (Chicago, 1992).

8. Roderyk Lange, *The Nature of Dance: An Anthropological Perspective* (London, 1975) and Paul Spencer, ed., *Society and the Dance* (Cambridge, 1985) are exceptions, bringing broad but for the most part ahistorical perspectives to their discussion of social meanings attached to human dancing.

9. Felicitas D. Goodman, *Where the Spirits Ride the Wind* (Bloomington, Ind., 1990), p. 17, describes how she used hypnosis—not dance—to induce trance in American college students, who had nothing to report on recovering ordinary consciousness. She concluded: "The trance experience itself is a vacuous neurophysiological event that receives content only from signals present in the respective cultures."

10. Kaj Bjorkquist, "Ecstasy from a Physiological Point of View," in Nils G. Holm, ed., *Religious Ecstasy* (Uppsala, 1982), pp. 74–86; I. M. Lewis, *Ecstatic Religion,* 2nd ed. (London, 1971), pp. 10–38; Charles T.

Tait, ed., *Altered States of Consciousness* (New York, 1969), pp. 9–22; Erika Bourguignon, "Trance Dance," *Dance Perspectives,* 35 (1968) 15–60; Felicitas D. Goodman, *Speaking in Tongues* (Chicago, 1972), pp. 60–79.

11. REM signifies "rapid eye movement" of the sort that occurs during this phase of sleep. For the comparison of REM sleep with trance see Felicitas Goodman, Jeanette H. Henney, and Esther Pressel, *Trance and Hallucination: Three Field Studies of Religious Experience* (New York, 1974), p. 346.

12. Neanderthal burials constitute the earliest archaeological attestation of concern for the departed. How complete Neanderthal mastery of language was is of course unknown, but it may have been comparable to that of *Homo sapiens.* See Brian Hayden, "The Cultural Capacities of Neanderthals: A Review and Re-Evaluation," *Journal of Human Evolution,* 24 (1993) 113–146.

13. This can even be routinized, so that on a given day at a meeting of the Umbanda in Brazil the cult leader announces in advance what spirit will possess the participants—child, wicked person, slave, saint, or hero as the case may be. See Goodman, Henney, and Pressel, *Trance, Healing and Hallucination,* p. 135.

14. S. M. Shirkogoroff, *Psycho-Mental Complex of the Tungus* (London, 1935) as quoted in Lewis, *Ecstatic Religion,* pp. 46–47.

15. The classic (and admirably learned) work on shamanism is Mircea Eliade, *Shamanism: Archaic Techniques of Ecstasy* (Princeton, 1964). This is a translation, with minor amendment, of a French edition of 1951.

16. See, for example, the exact hour by hour account of an all-night healing trance-dance in Richard Katz, *Boiling Energy: Community Healing among the Kalahari Kung* (Cambridge, Mass., 1982), pp. 59–79.

17. Mark Nathan Cohen, *Health and the Rise of Civilization* (New Haven, 1989), pp. 55–74. Cohen argues persuasively that early farmers experienced a poorer diet and suffered from more disease than hunters and gatherers. The shift to food production, he suggests, was a response to "growing population, expansion into game-poor environments, and the disappearance of large game animals" (p. 56).

18. Karl Bucher, *Arbeit und Rhythmus,* 4th ed. (Leipzig and Berlin, 1909), pp. 28, 32, 33. This book offers many other examples of rhythmic field work in more or less egalitarian communities.

19. 2 vols. (Boston: Little, Brown, 1974).

20. Lawrence W. Levine, *Black Culture and Black Consciousness,* (New York, 1979), pp. 16–17, describes several instances of such mockery.

21. Bucher, *Arbeit und Rhythmus,* p. 102.

22. *Chicago Record Herald,* 10 January 1901, as quoted in Bucher, *Arbeit und Rhythmus,* p. 250.

23. Ibid., p. 440.

24. Zulu and Swazi societies were organized around age cohorts to a very considerable degree, but this was exceptional and connected with the radical militarization that Shaka Zulu carried through early in the nineteenth century. See Eileen Jensen Krige, *The Social System of the Zulus* (Pietermaritzburg, 1936) and Hilda Kufer, *An African Aristocracy: Rank among the Swazi of Bechuanaland* (Oxford, 1947). On initiation rites generally, see Frank W. Young, *Initiation Ceremonies: A Cross Cultural Study of Status Dramatization* (Indianapolis, 1965). This is a rather barren effort at statistical comparison and classification.

25. I rely on reading done long ago for these remarks on Sumerian priestcraft; see works cited in William H. McNeill, *The Rise of the West* (Chicago, 1963), pp. 40ff. The two most important were: Edouard Dhorme, *Les réligions de Babylonie et de l'Assyrie* (Paris, 1945) and Henri Frankfurt et al., *Before Philosophy* (Harmondsworth, 1941).

26. Robert R. Wilson, *Prophecy and Society in Ancient Israel* (Philadelphia, 1980), pp. 98–115, offers a recent, scholarly discussion of this first appearance of prophecy. Friedrich Ellermeier, *Prophetie in Mari und Israel* (Herzberg, 1968), translates the relevant texts.

27. I Kings 18.

28. J. F. K. Hecker, *The Dancing Mania of the Middle Ages* (New York, 1970), translates a pamphlet originally published by a German medical doctor in 1837. It remains the most comprehensive account of these popular dance outbreaks in western Europe, but cf. Eugene Louis Blackman, *Religious Dances in the Christian Church and in Popular Medicine* (London, 1952). For the possible role of ergot, see Mary Matossian, *Poisons of the Past: Epidemics and History* (New Haven, 1989). For an example of the elaboration of public rituals for protection against plague see Brian Pullen, *Rich and Poor in Renaissance Venice: The Social Institutions of a Catholic State to 1620* (Cambridge, Mass., 1971).

29. Simon Schama, *Citizens: A Chronicle of the French Revolution* (New York, 1989), p. 192

30. Mona Ozouf, *Festivals and the French Revolution* (Cambridge, Mass., 1988), p. 172.

31. Ibid., pp. 234–261.

32. See J. L. Talmon, "Social Prophetism in Nineteenth Century France: The Jewish Element in the Saint-Simonian Movement," *Commentary*, 26 (1958) 158–172.

33. I draw these particulars from a fine book by T. O. Ranger, *Dance and Society in East Africa, 1890–1970* (London, 1975).

34. Winston L. Barre, "Materials for a History of Studies of Crisis Cults: A Bibliographic Essay," *Current Anthropology*, 12 (1971) 3–44 assembled an enormous number of instances of this sort of behavior, in times long past as well as recently. For a narrative acount see Vittorio Lanternari, *The Religion of the Oppressed: A Study of Modern Messianic Cults* (New York, 1963).

35. Among the Senecas, beginning in 1799, Handsome Lake was inspired by dreams to preach a new, partly Christian religion that persists to the present. Doctrines meld Iroquois with Christian motifs; and four annual dances consolidate fellow-feeling. As a result of these reforms, the Senecas and other Iroquois tribes among whom the religion subsequently spread survived and have begun to assert themselves in white society much more successfully than most American Indian peoples. See *Encyclopedia Britannica*, s.v. "Handsome Lake Cult"; Anthony F. C. Wallace, *Religion: an Anthropological View* (New York, 1966), pp. 31ff.

36. See James Mooney, *The Ghost Dance Religion and the Sioux Outbreak of 1890,* abridged by A. F. C. Wallace (Chicago, 1965). The original was published as two stout volumes of the U.S. Bureau of Ethnology, *Annual Report, 1892–93* (Washington, D.C. 1896).

37. See Peter Worsley, *The Trumpet Shall Sound: A Study of "Cargo Cults" in Melanesia,* 2nd ed. (London, 1968) and Mircea Eliade, "Cargo Cults and Cosmic Regeneration," in Sylvia Thrupp, ed., *Millennial Dreams in Action* (The Hague, 1962), pp. 139–143.

38. Jane K. Cowan, *Dance and the Body Politic in Northern Greece* (Princeton, 1990), brings keen insight to the frictions between community-wide sentiment and sexual exhibitionism, as illustrated in dances in a village of Greek Macedonia in the 1980s. American TV programs had already become familiar in rural Greece by that time, and the tensions she describes were certainly affected by that fact. Older structures of authority and solidarity within Greek villages were profoundly disturbed

by their exposure to American pop culture, and the opening for sexual arousal through dance that Cowan detected was undoubtedly part of the general disruption of Greek peasant traditions.

## 4. Religious Ceremonies

1. I Kings 18.

2. Most experts accept the idea that ecstatic, collective forms of Hebrew prophecy derived from Canaanitish practices. See, for example, Robert R. Wilson, *Prophecy and Society in Ancient Israel* (Philadelphia, 1980); J. Lindblom, *Prophecy in Ancient Israel* (Philadelphia, 1962); Theodore H. Robinson, *Prophecy and the Prophets of Ancient Israel*, 3rd ed. (London, 1979); Emil G. Kraeling, *The Prophets* (Chicago, 1969).

3. I Samuel 19:24.

4. I Samuel 10:5–6.

5. I Samuel 10:11.

6. I Samuel 10:26; I Samuel ll:6.

7. I Samuel 8:7–18 is the strongest passage portraying Saul as usurper of God's rightful place; but the prevailing tone of the story makes him God's chosen agent, for instance, I Samuel 11:6. I am of course aware of the debates over how the biblical narrative may have been shaped by the effort of pious editors to reconcile different textual traditions, but feel it is safe to take these passages at face value as indication of real circumstances and extremes of behavior that were ambiguous at the time and became embarrassing afterwards. The fact that collective muscular expressions of prophetic ecstasy became embarrassing in later ages means, I think, that what editors preserved was indeed firmly attested by the original materials.

8. I Samuel 18:10.

9. I Samuel 22:2.

10. II Samuel 6:16–22; I Chronicles 15:28–29.

11. II Samuel 7:16.

12. II Samuel 12:1–25.

13. I Kings 11:4: "For it came to pass, when Solomon was old, that his wives turned away his heart after other gods: and his heart was not perfect with the Lord his God, as was the heart of David, his father."

14. The disasters that befell Jewish rulers and priesthoods betweeen 722 B.C., when the Assyrians conquered the Kingdom of Israel, and 586

B.C., when the Babylonians did the same to Judah, validated prophetic denunciations of their wickedness. The redefinition of God's will for men that ensued among the exiles in Babylon went a long way towards creating historic Judaism, and stands as a particularly successful and enormously influential example of how the emotional intensity of inspiration can be blended into ongoing tradition to maintain a living faith, even under what looked like very unfavorable conditions.

15. Cf., for example, C. Andre, "Ecstatic Prophecy in the Old Testament," in Nils G. Holm, ed., *Religious Ecstasy* (Uppsala, 1982), p. 200: "Orgiastic, vigorous ecstasy is alien to the Israelite prophets. On the other hand, it is found among false and non-Israelite prophets. The ecstasy of the YHWH prophets, primitive as well as classical, is characterized by a calm, sometimes paralytically calm, seeing and hearing of the word of YHWH, which they then feel compelled to forward." W. O. E. Oesterley, *The Sacred Dance: A Study in Comparative Folklore* (New York, 1923), though brief, is the fullest account of dancing in the Old Testament that I have discovered. He views prophetic ecstasy as an intensification of "normal processional" dances before the Ark (p. 108).

16. E. E. Dodds, *The Greeks and the Irrational* (Berkeley, 1951), pp. 69–77; Martin P. Nilsson, *A History of Greek Religion,* 2nd ed. (Oxford, 1967), pp. 206–207; Gilbert Murray, *Five Stages of Greek Religion,* 3rd ed. (New York, 1955), p. 27. These authors all deplore extreme behavior associated with these rites, showing themselves quite as squeamish as Old Testament scholars in dealing with the more violent emotions generated by keeping together in time. Two newer books escape this limitation: Henri Jeanmaire, *Dionysios, histoire du culte de Bacchus* (Paris, 1978) and Lillian B. Lawlor, *The Dance in Ancient Greece* (Middletown, Conn., 1965), pp. 76–85.

17. Acts 9:1–20; 10:10–16.

18. Acts 2:1–15.

19. Acts 8:14–17.

20. Acts 10:44–46.

21. Even so, glossolalia is seldom or never sustained for very long by any single person, and tends to wax and wane within each group of worshippers over time. See Felicitas D. Goodman, "Disturbances in the Apostolic Church: A Trance-Based Upheaval in Yucatan," in Felicitas D. Goodman, Jeanette H. Henney, and Esther Pressel, *Trance, Healing and Hallucination: Three Field Studies of Religious Experience* (New York, 1974), pp. 231 ff.

22. Eugene Louis Blackman, *Religious Dances in the Christian Church and in Popular Medicine* (London, 1952), p. 37.

23. Clement of Alexandria (d. 216) "Thou shalt dance in a ring, together with angels around Him," quoted in Blackman, *Religious Dances*, p. 19.

24. Speech 42, quoted in Blackman, *Religious Dances*, p. 29.

25. This is the view of Jean Claude Schmitt, *La raison des gestes dans l'occident médiéval* (Paris, 1990), pp. 86–92.

26. Blackman, *Religous Dances*, pp. 33–34.

27. Jean W. Sedlar, *India and the Greek World: A Study in the Transmission of Culture* (Totowa, N.J., 1980), pp. 234–264; Richard Garbe, *India and Christendom: The Historical Connections between Their Religions* (LaSalle, Ill., 1959).

28. As I remarked in Chapter One, trance induced by dance and prolonged muscular exertion may be the result of intervention of the para-sympathetic nervous system to protect the body from excessive strain. At any rate, the effect is to inhibit response to most external stimuli. By repressing reponse deliberately, as yogis seek to do, a similar (or perhaps identical) state can therefore be attained with considerably less bodily effort, and with correspondingly decreased arousal of group emotions. On sensory deprivation and trance, see Barbara W. Lex, "Physiological Aspects of Ritual Trance," *Journal of Altered States of Consciousness*, 2 (1975) 109–122.

29. The most famous example of crowd violence fomented and led by excited monks was the barbarous murder of the Neoplatonic philosopher Hypatia at Alexandria in 415.

30. See Carolyn Dietering, *The Liturgy as Dance and the Liturgical Dance* (New York, 1984), p. 35.

31. Schmitt, *La raison des gestes*, p. 126. My translation.

32. Walter Sorell, *Dance in Its Time*, (New York, 1981), p. 11.

33. Schmitt, *La raison des gestes*, p. 319. My translation.

34. The monks of Mt. Athos were the protagonists of the new style of holiness. They probably borrowed their techniques for inducing the vision of God from Moslem dervishes—one of many instances in which ecstatic behavior has crossed confessional and cultural boundaries. On hesychasm see Jean Meyendorff, *St. Grégoire Palamas et la mystique orthodoxe* (Paris, 1959). The Rhineland mystics, of whom Ruysbroeck was one, may well have been the most westerly participants in a contagious upwelling of mystical behavior, centered in Moslem lands and

ultimately deriving from India. But devotees of different faiths were not inclined to admit borrowing from unbelievers and were perhaps seldom aware of the striking commonalities betrayed in details of their ascetic exercises.

35. Hans Peter Clasen, *Anabaptism: A Social History, 1525–1618* (Ithaca, N.Y., 1972), records a number of outbreaks of ecstatic and violent behavior, but also shows how Anabaptist pastors strove to suppress such outbreaks in hope of forestalling the brutal and violent repression that civil authorities repeatedly used against them.

36. Richard Gough, *The History of Myddle* (Ascot, Berks., 1979) offers an interesting insight into the social importance of pew ownership in an early eighteenth-century English parish, for he organizes his account of the gentry families of the parish according to which pew they rented in his church. The spread of pews was gradual, starting as a privilege for a few, and becoming available to everybody only in course of the nineteenth century. In contrast, enthusiastic revival meetings and upstart store-front churches always did without the constraint of pews. This is also true of Orthodox churches, where worshippers remain on their feet and often move about during services, coming forward to light a votive candle, for instance, or bowing to the ground at the back of the church in private prayer while the liturgy proceeds.

37. A. Ronald Sequeira, *Klassische indische Tanzkunst und die christliche Verkündigung* (Freiburg, 1978), p. 253.

38. Lynn Matluk Brooks, *The Dances and Processions of Seville in Spain's Golden Age* (Kassel, 1988), pp. 71–78 and *passim*.

39. I failed to find anything more than cursory mention of muscular manifestations of the Spirit among recent authorities whose books I consulted. J. F. McGregor and Barry Reay, eds., *Radical Religion in the English Revolution* (London, 1984), devote a few sentences to muscular outbreaks of enthusiasm among Ranters, Quakers, and others without explaining whether or not the behavior took rhythmic form. Other scholars had nothing to say; see, for example, Richard L. Greaves, *Deliver Us from Evil: The Radical Underground in Britain, 1660–1663* (New York, 1986) and Patrick Collinson, *The Religion of Protestants: The Church in English Society 1559–1625* (London, 1985).

40. McGregor and Reay, eds., *Radical Religion in the English Revolution*, pp. 141–164. Muscular manifestation of inspiration continued to break out among some Quaker groups throughout the eighteenth century. One such community, reinvigorated by contact with French Hu-

guenot "prophets," attracted Ann Lee, who subsequently founded the Shaker sect in the United States. See Ronald A. Knox, *Enthusiasm: A Chapter in the History of Religion* (Oxford, 1950).

41. Gershom G. Scholem, *Sabbatai Sevi, the Mystical Messiah, 1626–1676* (Princeton, 1973), authoritatively dismisses any connection between Sabbatai Sevi and English messianic expectations. His claim did, nonetheless, arouse considerable interest in England, as attested by John Evelyn, *The History of Sabatai Sevi, the Supposed Messiah of the Jews* (Augustan Reprint Society, #13; Los Angeles, 1968).

42. Louis Jacobs, *Hasidic Prayer* (London, 1972) provides careful detail and a judicious weighing of fragmentary evidence of how Hasidic enthusiasts actually worshipped.

43. Jacobs, *Hasidic Prayer*, pp. 56, 60.

44. Martin Buber, *Tales of the Hasidim: The Early Masters* (New York, 1947), p. 171. On Hasidism see also Bernard D. Weinryb, *The Jews of Poland: A Social and Economic History of the Jewish Community in Poland from 1100 to 1800* (Philadelphia, 1973), pp. 262–303.

45. James Billington, *The Icon and the Axe, An Interpretive History of Russian Culture* (New York, 1966), p. 153; Robert O. Crummey, *The Old Believers and the World of Anti-Christ: The Vyg Community and the Russian State, 1694–1855* (Madison, Wisc., 1970). One sect of Old Believers, after migrating to Canada, customarily expressed collective protest against acts and policies of public authorities by stripping off their clothes and parading naked.

46. And in the twentieth century as well. In the late 1930s I once dropped in on such a sect; it was one of Father Divine's so-called Heavens in New York City. Music, singing, and muscular movements among the congregation soon set the rather dingy Heaven—an upstairs loft in Harlem—to rocking; and every so often individual members of the congregation experienced trance and babbled unintelligibly for a few minutes, only to recover and rejoin the enthusiastic singing as before. In this instance, the driving rhythm of a small but accomplished brass band seemed to me to regulate the level of excitement. When ecstatic seizures multiplied, the band interrupted its playing and a preacher took over; then, when the excitement diminished, the instrumental music, singing, and vigorous bodily movement resumed until trance behavior again started to break out.

47. Amos Taylor as quoted by Lawrence Foster, *Religion and Sexuality* (New York, 1981), pp. 35–64; see also Stephen J. Stein, *The Shaker Experience in America: A History of the United Society of Believers*

(New Haven, 1992); Doris Faber, *The Perfect Life: The Shakers in America* (New York, 1974).

48. Leonard J. Harrington and Davis Bitton, *The Mormon Experience* (New York, 1978), pp. 218–219.

49. Sermon of 29 December 1850, as published in *Desert News*, 11 January 1851, and quoted by Ronald W. Walker, "'Going to Meeting' in Salt Lake City's Nineteenth Ward: A Microanalysis," in Davis Bitton and M. U. Beecher, eds., *New Views of Mormon History* (Salt Lake City, 1987), p. 145.

50. Douglas D. Alder, "The Mormon Ward: Congregation or Community?" *Journal of Mormon History*, 5 (1978) 70.

51. Goodman, "Disturbances in the Apostolic Church," in Goodman, Henney, and Pressel, *Trance, Healing and Hallucination*, pp. 231–380, describes the tribulations of Pentecostalists in an Indian village in Yucatan (Mexico), who confidently expected the end of the world in 1970 and then had to reinterpret the episode, attributing it to Satanic inspiration. Her account is both sympathetic and insightful. For an account of a similar group on the Caribbean island of St. Vincent, see Erika Bourguignon, *Religion: Altered States of Consciousness and Social Change* (Columbus, Ohio, 1973), pp. 233–260.

52. On Pentacostalism see Robert M. Anderson, *Vision of the Disinherited: The Making of American Pentacostalism* (New York, 1979); David Martin, *Tongues of Fire: The Explosion of Protestantism in Latin America* (Oxford, 1990); Susan Rose and Quentin Schultze, "The Evangelical Awakening in Guatemala: Fundamentalist Impact on Education and the Media," in Martin E. Marty and R. Scott Appleby, eds., *Fundamentalisms and Society* (Chicago, 1993), pp. 415–451.

53. Pedro McGregor, *The Moon and Two Mountains: The Myths, Ritual and Magic of Brazilian Spiritualism* (London, 1966); Esther Pressel, "Umbanda," in Goodman, Henney, and Pressel, *Trance, Healing and Hallucination* pp. 123–217.

54. Bengt G. M. Sundkler, *Bantu Prophets in South Africa*, 2nd ed. (Oxford, 1961), p. 198. Sundkler also published an updated and extended account of recent religious affairs in South Africa, entitled *Zulu Zion and some Swazi Zionists* (London, 1976).

55. Sundkler, *Bantu Prophets*, p. 199.

56. Ibid., pp. 281, 330.

57. On Shaka's military arrangements see Donald R. Morris, *The Washing of the Spears* (New York, 1965); Eileen Jensen Krige, *The*

*Social System of the Zulus* (Pietermaritzburg, 1936). I have no information about how Shemba's church has fared since 1976, when Bengt Sundkler's reports on his field studies ended.

58. For a useful discussion of the importance of transcending tribal quarrels, see Fred M. Donner, *The Early Islamic Conquests* (Princeton, 1981), pp. 267–281. The only conceivable test for my notion that I can think of would be to measure the physiological changes, if any, that public prayer arouses among Moslems today. If they resemble changes induced by more strenuous and excited dance, then one could assume that emotional effect of consolidating comradeship and fellow feeling would be similar or the same. But no one has yet measured what dancing does to the human body; moreover, difficulties in doing so are immense inasmuch as the chemical and electrical changes involved are extremely complex, and how can one measure them without interrupting, or at least altering, the dance—or the prayer?

59. As translated by Edward Fitzgerald, "The Rubaiyat of Omar Khayyam," quatrain 59: "The Grape that can with logic absolute / The Two and Seventy jarring sects refute."

60. Louis Massignon, *Essai sur les origines du lexique technique de la mystique mussulmane* (Paris, 1968); Goren Ogen, "Religious Ecstasy in Classical Sufism," in Nils G. Holm, ed., *Religious Ecstasy* (Uppsala, 1983), pp. 226–240.

61. I once witnessed such a ceremony in Rockefellar Chapel on the campus of the University of Chicago and can testify to its hypnotic effect on an audience mostly, but not entirely, composed of unbelievers. Many Turks and other Moslems from the city had gathered for the occasion, but few of them were conspicuously pious.

62. I lived within a block of Elijah Mohammed's Temple No. 2 in Chicago for almost twenty years, and had an outsider's ringside seat on this remarkable and very rapid transformation.

63. On dervish mysticism the works of R. A. Nicholson, *Studies in Islamic Mysticism* (Cambridge, 1921) and A. J. Arberry, *Sufism* (London, 1950) are still authoritative. The best overview of the transformation of Islam by dervish piety is Marshall G. S. Hodgson, *The Venture of Islam*, vol 2, *The Expansion of Islam in the Middle Period*, (Chicago, 1974). For a provocative perspective on the historic importance of what he calls "religious internationals"—Moslem, Buddhist, and Christian—in early modern centuries see S. A. M. Adshead, *Central Asia in World History* (London, 1963), pp. 150–174.

64. A. Ronald Sequeira, *Klassische indische Tanzkunst und die christliche Verkündigung* (Freiburg, 1978), pp. 39–176, offers an admiring and perhaps also uncritical account of the history of sacred dancing in India.

65. The Hare Krishna sect that reached the United States in 1965 is a direct offspring of Chaitanya's movement. Members supported themselves by selling magazines and the like in public places, or by begging. They live communally and spend many hours each day dancing and chanting in honor of Krishna, hoping to attain esctatic union with him. See J. Stillson Judah, "The Hare Krishna Movement," in Irving I. Zaretsky and Mark P. Leone, eds., *Religious Movements in Contemporary America* (Princeton, 1971), pp. 463–478.

66. For Indian and Hindu history in general Charles Eliot, *Hinduism and Buddhism: An Historical Sketch*, 3 vols. (London, 1921) is impressively perspicacious. A. L. Basham, *The Wonder That Was India* (London, 1954) is another shorter, more recent, and judicious synthesis. For Chaitanya, see Melville T. Kennedy, *The Chaitanya Movement* (Calcutta, 1925).

67. T'ai Tsu (r. 1368–98), the founder of the Ming dynasty, was born into a poor peasant family and became a Buddhist monk in his youth. He then joined armed rebels and ended up on the imperial throne, after driving the Mongols from China. Having gained power, however, he broke with his fellow sectarians and adopted the upper-class, Confucian way as his own.

68. Joseph W. Esherick, *The Origins of the Boxer Uprising* (Berkeley, 1987) and Victor Purcell, *The Boxer Uprising: A Background Study* (Cambridge, 1963) are both excellent. For distinctly dubious histories of Buddhist sectarian muscular exercises in the deeper past see Michael Minnick, *The Wisdom of Kung Fu* (New York, 1974) and Axel Anneville, *T'ai Chi: La gymnastique chinoise* (Paris, 1974).

69. On Confucian rites and their intersection with other forms of religion in China see Arthur P. Wolf, ed., *Religion and Ritual in Chinese Society* (Stanford, 1974); Wing-Tsit Chan, *Religious Trends in Modern China* (New York, 1969); C. K. Yang, *Religion in Chinese Society* (Berkeley, 1967); and Herbert Fingarette, *Confucius: The Secular as Sacred* (New York, 1972).

70. This figure comes from a glossy publication of Soka Gakkai International entitled *Waves of Peace towards the New Century*, p. 1. Other estimates are even higher. *Time Magazine* of 1 August 1960,

p. 60, put the total at no less than sixteen million, but this was clearly an exaggeration.

71. I rely on James White, *The Sokagakkai and Mass Society* (Stanford, 1970) and H. Neill McFarlane, *Rush Hour of the Gods* (New York, 1967) for these remarks. As McFarlane points out, acute strains in Japanese society caused a large number of other sects to come into being, beginning as early as 1838 and burgeoning—the rush hour of the gods—immediately after World War II. All had roots in Buddhist sectarianism; but none has come close to matching the success of Soka Gakkai.

# 5. Politics and War

1. See Norbert Elias, *The Court Society* (New York, 1983).

2. Equipping officers with large-gauge .45 inch calibre pistols became standard in the U.S. Army when smaller bullets proved incapable of stopping such Moro attacks, even though the charging warriors had only hand weapons at their disposal.

3. Tacitus, *Germania*, 24. Church and Brodribb trans.

4. Anonymous British report quoted in Andrew P. Vayda, *Maori Warfare* (Wellington, 1969), p. 62. New Zealand rugby teams prepare for their matches in world competition by doing the same today.

5. Judith L. Hanna, "African Dance and the Warrior Tradition," in Ali A. Mazrui, ed., *The Warrior Tradition in Modern Africa* (Leiden, 1977), pp. 111–133.

6. Ross Hassig, *Aztec Warfare: Imperial Expansion and Political Control* (Norman, Okla., 1988), p. 33.

7. Fray Bernardino de Sahagun, *General History of the Things of New Spain* (Santa Fe, N.M., 1979), part IX, "Kings and Lords", p. 55.

8. As quoted in Gertrude P. Kurath and Samuel Marti, *Dances in the Anahuac: The Choreography and Music of Pre-Cortesian Dances*, Viking Fund Publications in Anthropology #38 (New York, 1964), pp. 63–64.

9. For an interesting but somewhat superficial comparison of Spartans and Zulus see W. S. Ferguson, "The Zulus and the Spartans: A Comparison of Their Military Systems," *Harvard African Studies*, 2 (1918) 197–234.

10. Miguel Leon-Portilla, *Aztec Thought and Culture* (Norman, Okla., 1963), p. 103. According to Friedrich Katz, *The Ancient Amerin-*

*dian Civilizations* (London, 1972), p. 167, in the final decade of the Aztec empire as many as 15,000 persons were sacrificed every year.

11. Jacques Soustelle, *Daily Life of the Aztecs on the Eve of the Spanish Conquest* (Stanford, 1970), p. 243, quoting an Indian convert to Christianity.

12. Military systems aimed at capturing enemies were widespread. Nearly always the captives were put to work as slaves, or incorporated into the victor's society in some other way. The bloodthirsty Caribs, for instance, aimed to kill adult males and capture women and boys who were needed to maintain Carib numbers. See Jonathan Haas, *The Anthropology of War* (Cambridge, 1990), p. 155. Geoffrey Parker, *The Military Revolution* (Cambridge, 1988), p. 118, goes so far as to say of southeast Asia, America, and sub-Saharan Africa that "native wars in these areas were almost always fought to enslave enemies rather than to exterminate them." In general, this policy made sense when population shortages limited what could be done. Killing or sacrificing enemies made sense only when population surpluses pressed against available resources. For interesting remarks on how this balance worked out in Polynesia, see Andrew Peter Vayda, *War in Ecological Perspective* (New York, 1976).

13. For instance, A. Heidel, ed., *The Epic of Gilgamesh and Old Testament Parallels* (Chicago, 1946), Tablet I, column ii: "Gilgamesh leaves no son to his father," "Gilgamesh leaves no virgin to her lover"; nonetheless, "Gilgamesh is the shepherd of Uruk."

14. Ibid., Tablet III, columns i and ii tells how Gilgamesh went to the temple to seek advice and protection before starting out for the cedar forest.

15. Ibid., Tablet III, column iv: "The craftsmen sat down and held a conference; great weapons they cast, axes of three talents each they cast. Great swords they cast with blades of two talents each." All this was in preparation for an expedition to the cedar forest to cut logs.

16. With perhaps one exception. Naram Sin's stele shows him wearing a headdress that is associated with what gods' wore in other representations, and he may have claimed divinity. If so, his example was not followed afterwards until the time of Alexander of Macedon and his Hellenistic successors. They toyed with Egyptian ideas of divine rulership, as Naram Sin may also have been doing.

17. The gap between Communist Chinese ideals of thought control and American notions of civil rights that currently troubles the diplo-

matic relations between the two governments reflects the difference between the Chinese tradition of merging religion with politics and our separation of church and state.

18. A second famous work of art, the so-called Standard of Ur, also shows foot soldiers in step; but they form a single file, and the parallelism of their limbs might be an artistic convention. Still, this may count as a probable additional evidence of Sumerian infantry drill.

19. Yigael Yadin, *The Art of War in Biblical Lands* (New York, 1973), pp. 150–151 first advanced the view that compound bows, introduced perhaps by Sargon of Akkad, revolutionized warfare in ancient Mesopotamia.

20. Ibid., pp. 295–303.

21. For interesting details about how the Assyrians introduced cavalry into their armies under Assurnasirpal II (r. 883–859 B.C.) see Florence Malbran-Labat, *L'armée et l'organisation militaire de l'Assyrie* (Geneva-Parnius, 1982), pp. 61ff.

22. The Lippizzaner horses, long maintained for ceremonial purposes by the Hapsburgs and still existing in Vienna, do move in unison and keep time to music; but their riders achieve this result only by keeping very tight control over their mounts. Long training is needed to get the horses to obey so precisely; and the horses never learn to keep time spontaneously.

23. Edward Shaughnessy, "Historical Perspectives on the Introduction of the Chariot into China," *Harvard Journal of Asiatic Studies*, 48 (1988) 180–237.

24. Sun Tzu, *The Art of War* (Oxford, 1963), p. 58.

25. Ralph D. Sawyer, trans., *The Seven Military Classics of Ancient China* (Boulder, Co., 1993), pp. 266–267.

26. I take these dates from Samuel Griffith's introduction to Sun Tzu, *The Art of War*, pp. 9, ll.

27. Frank A. Kierman, Jr. and John K. Fairbank, eds., *Chinese Ways of Warfare* (Cambridge, Mass., 1974), pp. 5, 64; D. Twitchett and Michael Loewe, eds., *The Cambridge History of China*, I (Cambridge, 1986), pp. 24–25.

28. For the rugby scrum model see Victor Davis Hanson, *The Western Way of War: Infantry Battle in Classical Greece* (Oxford, 1989), and Victor Davis Hanson, ed., *Hoplites: The Classical Battle Experience* (London, 1991), pp. 63–84. For individual dueling see Peter Krantz, "The Nature of Hoplite Battle," *Classical Antiquity*, 4 (1985) 50–61.

The two premier authorities remain noncommittal: P. A. Greenhalgh, *Early Greek Warfare: Horsemen and Chariots in the Homeric and Archaic Age* (Cambridge, 1973), p. 74; W. Kendrick Pritchett, *The Greek State at War* (Berkeley, 1974), I, 144–154. For ritual aspects of phalanx fighting see W. R. Connor, "Early Greek Warfare as Symbolic Expression," *Past and Present,* 19 (1988) 3–29.

29. Hanson, ed., *Hoplites*, pp. 5–6; Robin Osborne, *Classical Landscape with Figures* (London, 1987), pp. 137–64; A. M. Snodgrass, "The Hoplite Reform and History," *Journal of Hellenic Studies,* 85 (1965) 110–122; Marcel Detienne, "La phalange: Problèmes et controversies," in Jean-Paul Vernant, *Problèmes de la guerre en Grèce ancienne* (Paris, 1967), pp. 119–142.

30. Charles Hignett, *Xerxes' Invasion of Greece* (Oxford, 1963).

31. Chrysis Pelekidis, *Histoire de l'éphebie attique* (Paris, 1962), pp. 75–85; C. A. Forbes, "Expanded Uses of the Greek Gymnasium," *Classical Philology,* 40 (1945) 32–42; Jean Delorme, *Gymnasium: Etude sur les monuments consacrés a l'éducation en Grèce* (Paris, 1960), pp. 26–30

32. Greenhalgh, *Early Greek Warfare,* p. 74.

33. Pierre Ducray, *Guerre et guerriers dans la Grèce antique* (Freibourg, 1985), p. 72, my translation.

34. *History,* V, 69–70. Crawley trans.

35. *Life of Lycurgus,* 21–22. Dryden's trans.

36. J. F. Lazenby, *The Spartan Army* (Warminster, 1985), p. 26.

37. Pritchett, *The Greek State at War,* II, 216.

38. Paul A. Rahe, *Republics Ancient and Modern* (Chapel Hill, 1992), pp. 143–152 translates some of these songs.

39. Pritchett, *The Greek State at War,* IV, 63.

40. Borimir Jordan, *The Athenian Navy* (Berkeley, 1975), pp. 103–106 explains the need for rowing practice. For a convincing reconstruction of how the oars were arranged in three tightly compacted tiers see J. S. Morrison and J. F. Coates, *The Athenian Trireme: The History and Reconstruction of an Ancient Greek Warship* (Cambridge, 1986).

41. Two of my friends, who rowed in modern racing shells, recalled having ambivalent feelings toward other crew members. As they remembered it, irritation when someone flubbed an oar mingled with elation when all went well. An additional consideration: emotional response to keeping time together may thrive only among larger numbers than the eight of a modern racing shell. I find it hard to imagine that eight men,

lined up to drill all by themselves, would react in the way a platoon of forty does; but in the absence of physiological or psychological observations and tests no one can say for sure.

42. Pritchett, *The Greek State at War*, II, 228; Arthur Ferrill, *The Origins of War: From Stone Age to Alexander the Great* (London, 1985), pp. 159–161.

43. I consulted a French translation of Aelianus Tacticus, *La milice des Grècs et Romains*, Louis de Machault, trans. (Paris, 1605).

44. H. W. Parke, *Greek Mercenary Soldiers* (Oxford, 1933), is a classic. But neither Parke nor such authorities as F. E. Adcock, *The Greek and Macedonian Art of War* (Berkeley, 1957); John K. Anderson, *Military Theory and Practice in the Age of Xenophon* (Berkeley, 1970); and Donald W. Engels, *Alexander the Great and the Logistics of the Macedonian Army* (Berkeley, 1978), have much to say about drill.

45. Eric Birley, *The Roman Army: Papers, 1929–1986* (Amsterdam, 1988), argues that Vegetius wrote in the 440s; but Vegetius is more commonly dated about half a century earlier.

46. Quoted from G. R. Watson, *The Roman Soldier* (London, 1974), p. 54.

47. Vegetius, *Rei Militari Instituta*, 2:28.

48. Vegetius claims to base his account on writings by Cato the Censor and other worthies of the Republic and early empire. But, according to William Smith, *Classical Dictionary* (London, 1866), s.v., Vegetius: "The value of the work is much diminished by the fact that usages of periods the most remote from each other have been mixed together in one confused mass, and not unfrequently, we have reason to suspect, are blended with arrangements that never existed except in the fancy of the author."

49. We happen to be informed that in 107 B.C. Marius called on gladiators to teach his newly raised landless recruits how to use their weapons. Lawrence Keppie, *The Making of the Roman Army: From Republic to Empire* (London, 1984), p. 65. On Roman training see also H. M. D. Parker, *The Roman Legions* (Oxford, 1928), p. 226.

50. Armored cavalrymen, possessing efficient bows and a new breed of big horses strong enough to carry the extra weight of armor, appeared on the Danube frontier as early as Hadrian's time (r. 117–138 A.D.). The Romans promptly began to imitate and match these newly formidable barbarians with heavy cavalry of their own. Yvon Garlan, *War in the Ancient World: A Social History* (London, 1974), p. 122.

51. Arthur Ferrill, *The Fall of the Roman Empire: The Military Explanation* (London, 1988) offers a recent summary.

52. Western knights preferred spear and sword to the bows used by cataphracts of the East, thus renewing a bias in favor of hand-to-hand combat that had prevailed among Homer's heroes as well as among Greek and Roman infantrymen. Conventional definitions of courage may have had something to do with this phenomenon. For example, Euripides, *Heracles* 2, 62–64: "The bow in no proof of manly courage; no, your real man stands firm in the ranks and dares to face the gash the spear makes," as quoted by Garlan, *War in the Ancient World*, p. 128. Perhaps skills needed for making compound bows were also lacking. In addition, the prevalence of wooded terrain in northern Europe, when knighthood first established itself, may have reduced the bow's military effectiveness.

53. Royal bodyguards sometimes marched in step, but such ceremonial display had little relevance for actual fighting. For instance, Hsuan-Tsang, a Buddhist pilgrim to India, records that the mighty king Harsha (r. 606–647) had a bodyguard that marched in step to tap of drum: Samuel Beal, *The Life of Huien Tsiang* (London, 1911), p. 173. But Indian warfare, as elsewhere, was a matter of cavalry clashes, supplemented by infantry bowmen in open order, plus elephants and chariots. P. C. Chakravarti, *The Art of War in Ancient India* (Delhi, 1972), p. 123 and *passim*.

54. William Wayne Farris, *Heavenly Warriors: The Evolution of Japan's Military, 500–1300* (Cambridge, Mass., 1992), p. 15.

55. It is interesting to recognize that the Hussites used wagons in much the same way in Bohemia between 1420 and 1434, allowing rebellious commoners and mere infantry to resist knightly attack. The Visigoths, who invaded the Roman empire in 378 A.D. from the Russian steppeland, also sometimes used wagons for defense in the field. Perhaps, therefore, there was a long-standing tradition of cart warfare on the Eurasian steppes that Ch'i Chi-Kuang adapted for his purposes; but if so, any literary traces are so scattered that they have not been noticed by historians.

56. James Millinger, *Ch'i Chi-Kuang: Chinese Military Official* (PhD diss., Yale University, 1968), p. 134. Everything I know about Ch'i Chi-Kuang derives from this excellent study, which deserves far more attention than it has yet received.

57. Joseph Needham et al., *Science and Civilization in China*, V, Part

7, *Military Technology: The Gunpowder Epic* (Cambridge, 1986) settles the question of Chinese priority with completely convincing detail.

58. Justus Lipsius, with whom Maurice had studied, was perhaps the primary influence behind the return to antiquity. He held that correct discipline for armies was discoverable from Roman practices and wrote a book in 1595 to prove it, entitled *De Militia Romana libre quinque: Commentarius ad Polybium.* See Gerhard Ostreich, *Geist und Gestalt der frühmodernen Staaten,* (Berlin, 1969), pp. 12–34.

59. Notebooks kept by Maurice's cousin and aide, Johann of Nassau, reveal how broadly the reformers probed the past for helpful hints. Johann transcribed long passages, made diagrams, and commented on his reading from a great many Byzantine, Roman and Greek authors. See Werner Halbweg, ed., *Die Heeresreform der Orianer: Das Kriegsbuch des Grafen Johann von Nassau-Siegen* (Wiesbaden, 1973). This supplements his excellent earlier book: Werner Halbweg, *Die Heeresreform der Orianer und die Antike* (Berlin, 1941).

60. Service of a matchlock was indeed complex, requiring each soldier to insert powder, wad, bullet, and wad successively into the muzzle, tamp each down with a ramrod, then level the piece and pour a different sort of powder into the firing pan before attaching a smouldering match (held all the while in the left hand) to the trigger mechanism; and then aiming and, finally, pulling the trigger. Failure to perform any of these acts in the right sequence meant a misfire.

61. Jacob de Gheyn, *Wapenhandelinghe van Roers, Musquetten ends Spiessen, Achtervolgende de Ordre van Syn Excellentie Maurits, Prince van Orangie* (The Hague, 1607). I saw a fascimile edition printed in New York in 1971 with a very helpful commentary by J. B. Kist.

62. When I left the isolated anxiety of graduate school in 1941 to become a private in the Army of the United States, I personally experienced this odd sort of liberation and can attest that it was very real.

63. Bergen Evans, *Dictionary of Quotations* (New York, 1968), p. 259. Evans says that this remark is probably apocryphal, and is sometimes ascribed to William Pitt instead.

64. I Samuel 10:6.

65. Russian soldiers, themselves ex-peasants, defeated Pugachev's peasant rebellion (1773–1775). Their behavior showed how effectively army life and routines of drill could separate soldiers from their social origins. The so-called Peterloo massacre in England (1819) is a more clouded instance, for most of the British soldiers who fired at the rioters

on that occasion had only poverty in common with their urban victims; being primarily of rural origin, and many of the soldiers came from half-barbarous Scottish and Irish borderlands.

66. Mark Franko, "Renaissance Conduct Literature and the Basse Danse: The Kinesis of Bonne Grace," in R. C. Trexler, ed., *Persons in Groups: Social Behavior and Identity Formation in Medieval and Renaissance Europe* (Binghamton, N.Y., 1985), pp. 55–69; Walter Sorell, *Dance in Its Time* (New York, 1981), pp. 37ff.

67. Sir John Davies, "Orchestra, or a Poem on Dancing," reprinted in Gerald Bullet, ed., *Silver Poets of the Sixteenth Century* (New York, 1972), p. 52.

68. Roderyk Lange, *The Nature of Dance: An Anthropological Perspective* (London, 1975), p. 24.

69. The Duc de St. Simon's *Mémoires* show how one high nobleman chafed against the taming of the French nobility that Louis XIV achieved. See Norbert Elias, *The Court Society* (New York, 1983) and Norbert Elias, *Power and Civility* (New York, 1982).

70. M. D. Feld, "Middle Class Society and the Rise of Military Professionalism," *Armed Forces and Society*, 1 (1975) 409–442 was the first scholar to point out the convergence of courtly dance and military drill, as far as I know. His insight was boldly extended by Von Henning Eichberg, "Geometrie als Barocke Verhaltungsnorm: Fortifikation und Exerzitien," *Zeitschrift für historische Forschung*, 4 (1977) 17–50 to include gardening, classificatory natural history, and still other elements of European elite culture—all regarded as aspects of a coherent world view that emphasized unchanging orientation in geometrical space as against an evolutionary orientation in time that, he says, succeeded it after about 1770. This sort of *Geistesgeschichte* is perhaps suggestive, but it seems to me that the impact on human consciousness and actual behavior arising from shared rhythmic movements probably mattered more for the propagation of the spirit of geometry than did abstract, intellectualized impulses to systematize an understanding of the world.

71. Spanish weapons were (modestly) superior, but this would not have sufficed to secure victory for Cortez and Pizarro. Smallpox was their essential ally; and hard on the heels of smallpox other lethal diseases followed, destroying and demoralizing Amerindian peoples throughout the Americas. See William H. McNeill, *Plagues and Peoples* (New York, 1976), pp. 199–234.

72. For a sympathetic, nostalgic account, see Philip Mason, *A Matter of Honour: An Account of the Indian Army, Its Officers and Men* (London, 1974).

73. Samuel F. Scott, *The Response of the Royal Army in the French Revolution, 1787–1793* (New York, 1978).

74. Edmund Neuendorf, *Turnvater Jahn: Sein Leben und Werk* (Jena, 1928); Hannes Neuman, *Die deutsche Turnbewegung in der Revolution, 1848–49 und in der americanischen Emigration* (Stuttgart, 1968).

75. Fred E. Leonard and George B. Afflech, *A Guide to the History of Physical Education* (Philadelphia, 1947), pp. 114–129; Deobald B. Van Dalen, Elmer D. Mitchell, and Bruce L. Bennett, *A World History of Physical Education* (New York, 1953), pp. 221–228.

76. Peter C. McIntosh, *Physical Education in England since 1800*, 2nd ed. (London, 1968), pp. 98–120; Anne Bloomfield, "Drill and Dance as Symbols of Imperialism," in J. A. Mangan, ed., *Making Imperial Mentalities* (Manchester, 1990), pp. 74–95. Bloomfield says that Empire Day was shaped in imitation of Japanese Shinto rites honoring the emperor, but even if such were the intentions of those who started the celebration, I can attest on the basis of childhood memories that in Canada the American example of how to be patriotic prevailed.

77. Horst Ueberhorst, *Geschichte der Leibsübungen*, 5 vols. (Berlin, 1972–1976) V, 312ff.

78. Eugen Weber, "Gymnastics and Sports in Fin de Siècle France: Opium of the Classes?" *American Historical Review*, 76 (1971) 70–98.

79. See Brian Bond, ed., *Victorian Military Campaigns*, (London, 1967).

80. V. J. Parry, "La manière de combattre," in V. J. Parry and M. E. Yapp, eds., *Technology and Society in the Middle East* (London, 1975), pp. 218–256; David B. Ralston, *Importing the European Army: The Introduction of European Military Techniques and Institutions in the Extra-European World, 1600–1914* (Chicago, 1990); E. E. Ramsaur, *The Young Turks: Prelude to the Revolution of 1908* (Princeton, 1957); H. C. Armstrong, *Gray Wolf: The Life of Kemal Ataturk* (New York, 1933).

81. Noel Perrin, *Giving Up the Gun: Japan's Reversion to the Sword, 1543–1879* (Boulder, Co., 1979).

82. Ueberhorst, *Geschichte der Leibesübungen*, IV, 210ff.

83. Richard J. Smith, *Mercenaries and Mandarins: The Ever Victorious Army in Nineteenth Century China* (New York, 1978); Richard J.

Smith, "Foreign Training and China's Self-Strengthening: The Case of Feng Huang-shan," *Modern Asian Studies,* 10 (1976) 195–223.

84. Joseph W. Eshrick, *The Origins of the Boxer Uprising* (Berkeley, 1987).

85. Jonathan Kolatch, *Sports, Politics and Ideology in China* (New York, 1972), p. 80.

86. Which, as we saw in the previous chapter, had taken their modern form as a way of expressing the alliance sealed between the Hapsburg dynasty and Catholic Reform during the Thirty Years' War, 1618–1648.

87. Adolf Hitler, *Mein Kampf* (Boston, 1943), p. 41.

88. David Kertzer, *Ritual Politics and Power* (New Haven, Conn., 1988), pp. 163–168; J. Noakes and G. Pridham, eds., *A Documentary Reader: Nazism, 1919–45,* 2 vols. (Exeter, 1984), II, 410–415; J. P. Stern, *Hitler: The Führer and the People* (Berkeley, 1975), pp. 85–90.

89. Robert R. Taylor, *The Word in Stone* (Berkeley, 1974), pp. 33, 70.

90. See John Tolland, *Adolf Hitler* (New York, 1976), p. 135. Tolland gives no source for this mildly surprising story. After all, Hitler held the United States in very low esteem, and was not inclined to imitate American ways.

91. Stern, *Hitler,* p. 37.

# Conclusion

1. Richard Critchfield, *The Villagers: Changed Values, Altered Lives and the Closing of the Urban-Rural Gap* (New York, 1994), records his recent field studies of the recent disruption of village life styles in diverse parts of the world with thoroughly convincing specificity and detail.

# Index